AUTOBIOG BELIEVER: *Elusive Faith*

by
Gordon Durich

KDP ; Amazon Book Publishing

PRAISE

"I have had the honor of knowing Gordon David Durich (aka Gordie), and his search as a seeker of spiritual truth has been consistent, deep and is now bearing the fruit of fulfillment.

In this authentic and meaningful new writing, he brings an open-mindedness that shows up with distinction and as proof of his resilient and persistent search to discover, express and experience the true infinite and boundless self that abides within all. Gordon brings a universal consciousness to his writing, clearly indicative of the broader international flavor of his work, which reaches out to all, regardless of where you've been, where you are now, or where you are headed." *Reverend Doctor Sue Rubin, Minister Emeritus, Center for Spiritual Living, Westlake Village, California.*

"In *Autobiography of a Believer...Elusive Faith*, Gordon Durich brings his personal journey to faith to life in a powerful way. Seekers will be attracted to this book, as will people of faith. His writing is authentic, deeply personal and passionate." *Rev. Dr. Jim Lockard, author of "Being the Beloved Community: Spiritual Leadership to Master Change." Lyon, France.*

DEDICATION

This book is dedicated with love to my two mothers: my Mum and St. Mother Teresa, who represents the ultimate symbol of peace, love and compassion in my life. Above all, it is dedicated to my partner in life and Christ, my wife, Kitty.

ACKNOWLEDGMENTS

Profound thanks are due to the countless souls who listened to my stories; to my mentor, Craig Leener, for his constructive and creative support and encouragement; to Shari Hollander, my enthusiastic and skillful editor, and "Brother" John Conley, fellow artist-in-crime - and book "guru" and producer, without whom this book would not have been possible.

"Merely having an open mind is nothing. The object of opening the mind as of opening the mouth is to shut it again on something solid."

G.K. Chesterton

Serra Retreat, Malibu

"Whether a person believes in God or not, if someone is achieving extraordinary things, then I believe God is in that process."

Very Rev. John R. Hall, Dean of Westminster Abbey, London

PREFACE

Telling our stories has always been important. "When we deny our stories, they define us," says TED speaker Brené Brown. In the satiric observation of one of my favorite authors, Mark Twain: "Whenever you find yourself on the side of the majority, it is time to pause and reflect."

Considering that currently, the majority of the world's population are followers of Christianity that qualifies my religion as "the side of the majority." Therefore, I humbly offer up this book as my "pause and reflect," recounting mostly my own unique experiences of following the path of faith but also with commentary from muses and wiser minds than mine.

The seed of this writing project was planted during a men's weekend retreat open to both Catholics and unchurched believers alike—anyone who was curious about belief—at Serra Franciscan Retreat, a haven in the Malibu hills. Meditation, prayer and reflection replaced television with spacious amounts of time for reading while sipping cups of hot green tea. Early morning walkabouts around the beckoning labyrinth spiritually infused my budding literary efforts.

Since music influences and informs my creativity, I began jotting down those insights that rang true about my faith and belief with the working title of "Finding My Religion" (with a bow to R.E.M.'s *Losing My Religion)*.

The initial words were formed and sprouted to be sown further down the proverbial path, seeds not so much planted as tossed higgledy-piggledy into the universe over decades. Whispers from God in stolen moments on pews and park benches, scribbling copious notes on offering envelopes instead of cocktail napkins.

Until one typical Sunday morning at an Atmosphere Church service, Pastor Jim uttered three simple words that triggered my epiphany: *"Tell. Your. Story."* Adding, **"What is your story?** You don't need to know all the answers, but you need to know *your own story."*

Those profound words swept away the cobwebs of complacency from my writer's-blocked brain. He hadn't said my name, but it felt like he was talking directly to me: *Just write a bloody book, Gordo!*

"Follow Your Bliss"

In his book *Pathways to Bliss,* the renowned author Joseph Campbell posed and answered this existential question: *"What is it we are questing for? It is the fulfillment of that which is potential in each of us.* Questing for it is not an ego trip: it is an adventure to bring into fulfillment your gift to the world, which is yourself. There is nothing you can do that's more important than being fulfilled."

I realized that my bliss, my potential, my fulfillment, my gift to the world would be to write this book. In a sense, I was on what Campbell calls the hero's journey, exploring the idea that *when I believed, faith followed—* and not the other way 'round.

At that fateful Serra Retreat, Father Charlie Smiech told me: "As we share our faith experience with others, we, in turn, receive affirmation." Once I'd committed to writing my story, supportive messages began to show up.

Elvis Costello, a musician I'd long admired, provided an ad hoc soundtrack to my early efforts in his song *"Everyday I Write the Book."* Serendipitously serenading me, it was as if I was hearing the lyrics for the first time: "I'm a man with a mission on two or three editions." And don't we *all* write another *chapter* every day....

Serra

Retreat, Malibu.

INTRODUCTION

House of God
"My house shall be called a house of prayer" (Matthew 21:13).

I used to think that God dwelt only in churches. What my journey has shown me though is you don't need to have an *edifice complex*–an edifice per se—you just need yourself plus God. *I am the house that God dwells within.*

I've noticed that what often puts people off from pursuing their faith is thinking that they have to attend A Church in a traditional building. Preacher Rick Warren in his bestselling *The Purpose Driven Life* takes the right tack: "Buildings should be tools for ministry, not monuments."

Pastor Jim Crews of Atmosphere Church acknowledges though that being connected to others in a gathering does matter. Paraphrasing cosmologist Stephen Hawking (interestingly, a non-believer), Pastor Jim comments that "showing up (to church) is half the battle."

A bit like me in some respects, layperson and author Elizabeth Massie describes herself as "an ordinary, wondering-wandering unchurched believer who felt a Tap on her shoulder and decided not to ignore it." Her sentiments in her book *On the Outside Looking Up* are thought-provoking; and, ultimately, I found myself in agreement: "There isn't a private God Club in which only those with the one correct style of music or clothing or worship can take part."

It's All Good...It's All God
Regardless of your religion, having a belief in something positive, something larger than yourself is meaningful.

Rev. Michael Beckwith, founder of the "trans-denominational" LA-based Agape International Spiritual Center wrote: "My central message is not about religiosity or churchianity....living instead from...one's true nature of wholeness." Famed psychotherapist Carl Jung had this carved in

Latin over his door: "Bidden or not bidden, God is present," a reminder to those who entered of the presence of the spiritual in the mundane world.

I've learned that *A* Church is not what makes you *A* Christian. It's faith, prayer and devotion to God wherever *you* are, wherever *that* may be: indoors, in a tent, on a golf course, in a communal space, in a garden, on the beach, etc. God is *within* me. It's an inside job! In other words, *when–or wherever–you believe, faith follows.*

"For where two or three gather together as my followers, I am there among them." Humming along to folk trio Peter, Paul and Mary's iconic "*Wedding Song,*" were you aware of the composer's faith-based inspiration from Matthew 18:20? Paul Stuckey reverently enhanced the well-known quotation with "For whenever two or more of you are gathered in His name..."*There is love.*"

TABLE OF CONTENTS

I.   WONDERING

II.   WANDERING

Mystic in a Business Suit

Kathy

Last but not Louisest

MiseRecordia

Not to be Confused with...
A God Job

Passport to Massports

Church of the Open Mind

Panspirituality and Pascal
"For What It's Worth" (Stephen Stills
"Two Tickets to Paradise" (Eddie Money)
Meant to Be
Ah, Elusive Faith!

Faith and Hope, not Infamy

Religio-Catechesis

Still Searching

III.   **FOUND**

Of Boxes, Birds and Buddhists

Don't Just Do Something, Sit There!

Monk in a Mall
Finding My Religion (a nod and wink to R.E.M.)

PS
BONUS MATERIAL

Peace Be With You
In God We Trust
"Our Walks Are Prayers"...
Trivial But True
Famous and Faithful
Famous Buddhists...Did You Know?
Spiritual & Secular Playlist – Music for the Lyrical Soul
Movie Queue – Film and "Telly" (General)
Catholic Cinema
Famous Inspirations
Personal Spiritual Inspirations
Special Thanks
Resources – Useful Info.
Online Internet Sites
Resources – Get Involved
Lost In Translation (Glossary)
Resources – Read More
List of Illustrations & Pix
About The Author
Acknowledgements
Song Lyrics
Bibliography – Deeper Reading

I.   WONDERING

"The world will never starve for want of wonders but only for want of wonder."

- G.K. Chesterton

Born This Way

As a kid, while other boys were searching for tadpoles in creeks, I was searching for God. A precocious hunger for meaning and a yearning to belong led me to wander into empty houses of worship: Churches of England, Roman Catholic sanctuaries and Judaic synagogues as well as the glorious cathedrals of Melbourne, Australia. Like many seekers, I was equally curious, a budding panspiritual and theist. *Where did I belong?* Yusuf/Cat Stevens, a kindred soul, sang: "I was on the road to find out." Did comfort dwell within any of those walls? *Was anybody home?*

Family (Mind Your Own) Business

"Too often religion is blamed for being anti-science."

Bishop Robert Barron, The University Series (a multi-parish adult education program at Lent).

I had an inkling then that "churchy" people didn't always have it easy. More like *"salmon swimming upstream, going counterclockwise,"* as Deacon Jesse of St. Jude the Apostle once said to me. His piscine analogy resonated. I was more quietly ecclesiastically minded (sans being holier-than-thou) and that didn't sit well with the folks at home. Especially my Dad.

My father was an artist and an atheist who loved Isaac Asimov, Ray Bradbury and Arthur C. Clarke more than he seemed to love his only son. His head was in the stars, knowing every planet, but his earthly presence was firmly rooted in science, not speculation.

Dad's Higher Power was Science Almighty. Mum kept the extent of her belief in God under wraps (until later in life), a pattern that locked my family into a continual standoff. My sister was "Switzerland." She once wryly suggested one could pray to a rock. Or was it a tree? I took her big-picture meaning to be about Mother Nature, as in Psalm 23:2: "In green pastures you let me graze, to safe waters you lead me."

Blame it on undiagnosed Attention Deficit Hyperactive Disorder, but whenever a circle of Mum's church friends would gather at our house and pray before a meal, Dad would conveniently be somewhere else. *"Amen!"* he'd call out on autopilot from a few rooms away, usually in the kitchen, after being persuaded to pour the guests a plum brandy. Poor Dad. To appease Mum, he went along with churchgoing, feigning religiosity under the demure demand of "She-Who-Must-Be-Obeyed."

For appearances' sake and succumbing to the social pressure and expectations of friends and folks, I was stuffed into an uncomfortable suit and red clip-on bow tie and dragged off (rather like a dog on a leash) to Holy Trinity, a Serbian Orthodox church, a nod to my mater's heritage. Smells, bells and candle wax! Priests sporting dramatic black *kalimavkions*, waving incense and chanting hypnotically in Church Slavic. The only word I understood was *Christos*.

Those earlier agonizing influences aside, I recall a later conversation with my Old Man informing him that I was planning to go to church. Admonishing me, he scolded, "Don't become a fanatic!" Outraged, he all but wagged a finger in my face as if I were some kind of juvenile Jesus freak. Dumbfounded, I'd expected that attending a church service would have been greeted with a "good on ya" rather than a chastisement. Despite my devotion and naive theology, given those family dynamics, you could hardly describe *moi* as a "cradle" Catholic. If anything, I leaned more toward Anglican. Regardless, I believed that I was born to believe. In God.

"Ye shall know the truth and the truth shall make you free."

John 8:32

It's Never Too Late

For the record (and not so fond of labels except on record albums), yours truly identifies as a *born-again* Christian *without* broadcasting it. Born-again is a spiritual rebirth, being "born from above," open to God's grace. In my 60s, I rededicated my faith in Jesus Christ as my savior in a not-quite-traditional baptism in, of all places, a backyard swimming pool. Expiating my past sins was so cleansing, so liberating, that I had no desire to emerge from the cool water of that safe pool, reminiscent of Roger Daltrey's dive into the pool in the film version of *Tommy* (The Who's epic rock opera). *"I'm Free!"* I reminded myself: *Keep calm and trust in God, the Heavenly Father. He is good.*

16

My Earthly Father telling me off didn't dampen my curiosity one bit. The sound of his voice was like the schoolteacher in a *Charlie Brown* TV special: a muffled *wah-wah-wah*. God, on the other hand, was speaking directly *to me* in no uncertain terms!

I couldn't put into words why I'd always wrestled with a desire for something more, something deeper, that would move the dial of my emergent beliefs towards faith. More than once, while sitting on a solitary pew, I'd wondered if this was a sign that I was meant for the priesthood.

Even during those formative years, I'd unknowingly shared a principle with Founding Father Alexander Hamilton, namely: *"Those who stand for nothing, fall for anything."* And I stood for more—meaning walking the right path and trusting in "the man upstairs." I inherently believed in God, yet I believed there's "still much to believe in," *(Lost in Love,* Air Supply).

"The spiritual quest begins, for most people, as a search for meaning."
Marilyn Ferguson, The Aquarian Conspiracy

Abbey Roads

When left to my own devices, I was inexplicably drawn into those majestic, somewhat mysterious houses of worship Down Under. Man, what a field day I would've had if I'd been raised in the "City of Churches," as Adelaide—South Australia's attractive capital—had colloquially been dubbed. I'd gladly have indulged my heart with church-hopping the abbeys of Adelaide, which wasn't so much church-saturated, as known for its foundational religious freedom and spiritual diversity.

It wasn't just the awe-inspiring architecture that led this insatiable seeker to explore places of worship, but also their dramatic rituals that drew me in- as well as the soul-satisfying feeling of sanctuary.

Perfectly captured by Psalm 84: "How lovely is your dwelling place, O God I long to see your face," they con*spire*d to lead me on a journey rather than a destination of divinity and belonging to a godly home.

I found solace in a quote by *Keys of the Kingdom* novelist A.J. Cronin: "But always, if we have faith, a door will open for us, not perhaps one that we ourselves would ever have thought of, but one that will ultimately prove good for us."

17

"School's Out Forever"

Looking back contemplatively, I could say that my closest call with Catholicism was a fair dinkum act of God. It began routinely enough early one Monday morning, trudging to our old, red-brick Melbourne primary school, dragging our heavy school bags along the pavement—"just another brick in the wall" (subjugated à la Pink Floyd).

Gobsmacked, we stared in disbelief: overnight, our schoolhouse had been reduced to a pile of smoldering ashes! Slowly, the possibility dawned on us like those unruly kids in the Alice Cooper anthem: *"School's out forever!"* We gleefully shouted silent *Hallelujahs.*

I hated school and the mandatory early-morning assemblies in the quadrangle cheering "God Save The Queen!" I would rather have praised God than saved the Queen! (Akin to the irreverent Sex Pistols version, not the patriotic one.) Now that our primary education was burnt crumpet, was I to be home-schooled- or sent to one of those stuffy independent schools? "Parish" the thought. The uninhibited jubilation at our *learning-interruptus* was short-lived. Sobered by being shipped off to St. Something-or-Other, a nearby Catholic school in Box Hill.

The Lord works in mysterious ways. There, instead of our lovely, long-suffering schoolteachers, were strict Sisters. *Jesus, Mary and Joseph!* Nuns, for all intents and purposes—more intense than with a purpose! Back then, it seemed so odd to my eleven-year-old self. But, in hindsight, I prefer to see it as preordained, planting the seeds of my future faith. Or was it?

Though a troubled spirit, I was instantly drawn to the supposedly dreary Religious Instruction ("R.I"). Unlike my unruly classmates, I was fascinated by the theatricality of being taught by these women costumed in dramatic habits as well as by the pageantry of Catholicism. Raps on my knuckles from the sisters' rulers made it obvious that we defined "rapture" differently. I was the proverbial naughty schoolboy who'd apparently inherited Dad's latent A.D.H.D. When Isabelle Allende confessed in her autobiography, "I was expelled by the nuns when I was six," crikey, could I ever relate! Yours truly was older but apparently *not* wiser.

St. Something's nuns were unlike the gentle gentiles at St. Joseph's in Philadelphia that I'd heard about from Dr. James Mellon. To this day, he fondly remembers Sister Mary Michael, whom he credits with teaching him that *"God is everywhere. God is in your heart."* It's not a stretch to see this

18

philosophy in effect at his Global Truth Center, a Los Angeles spiritual community of love and unconditional acceptance, where he's the Founding Spiritual Director.

In contrast, even the austere edifice of St. Something-or-Other, which commanded the intersection of two busy Box Hill streets, was a lot like the visages of those intimidating nuns. Though, comfortingly, a large white statue of sweet Jesus stood out front with outstretched arms benignly directing traffic.

"Smells Like Teen Spirit" (Nirvana)

I wasn't a suggestible teenager, but I was very open-minded. More like a seeker with an identity crisis who had even surreptitiously considered converting to Hare Krishna to the chagrin of my long-suffering parents. I felt the peaceful message of these devotees clicked—to be of service—while chanting their eponymous mantra *Hare Krishna, Hare Krishna, Krishna Krishna, Hare Rama*. Not to mention, vegan meals costing next-to-nothing served at Gopals, their two cafes in the center of downtown Melbourne. The intoxicating scent of sweet *nag champa* incense mingled with *dal* and fragrant spices swirls through my memories of that time in that city.

While the other blokes from school were devouring Big "Maccas" (Aussie slang for McDonald's), my tucker comprised a pungent plateful of rice and veggies. Sitting alongside shaven-headed, sari-wearing Hare Krishna devotees, I chatted and chanted with these *soul*-mates. Despite my giveaway-gray school uniform, I did not feel out of place, sans the ubiquitous saffron robe and beads nor sporting a *tilaka* on my pimply forehead.

I, curious, scooped up their abundant ISKON books and pamphlets to learn about Krishna consciousness and the "superhuman" A.C. Bhakivdanta Swami Prabhupada. Read every single, bloody word. Cleared my bedroom bookshelf, replacing Dad's unread sci-fi paperbacks with a copy of *The Science of Self-Realization* by "A.C."

Was I being brainwashed as everyone (especially Dad) thought? No, I felt open to this new experience and loved its exotic vibe but certainly was not indoctrinated. The good vibes, thread of music and intense incense drew me in.

19

After all, if it was good enough for The Beatles to go Indian, it was good enough for this seeker of meaning. *Search for Liberation* featured a conversation between A.C., John and George—and, of course, the ubiquitous Yoko. Like her, those paperbacks were everywhere in the days of Hare Krishnas. They took to the streets from San Francisco to Sydney, Manhattan to Melbourne, with their beautiful bells and sweet songs of peace, tempting me to join in the parade. It was an experience of spiritual and communal liberty for this pubescent pilgrim.

Later stops on my assiduous spiritual path in Australia included the Divine Light Mission, headed by Guru Maharaji (aka Prem Rawat). The hypnotic tones of the vinyl LP *Home* not only wooed me with its nod to the Indian master but also melded with bloody fabulous songs and music! Spirited lyrics along the lines of "He's got all the answers" appealed to this impressionable, young Melbournian seeker.

Influences and introductions to other organized religions followed with unmitigated fervor and disorganization. Pentecostalism showed up in the shape of a turbo-tongued high school classmate with a take-*all*-prisoners attitude. Bubbly Beth dragged us along to a church-in-a-theatre in the 'burb of Kew (named after England's borough most likely) packed with parishioners who seemed to be under a collective religious spell. When they started speaking in tongues, I freaked out! This was way too confrontational for someone who did not understand what the heck was going on.

"Yabba-Dabba Do!" quipped Pastor Jim of Atmosphere, close-to-home, but more importantly, our *nondenominational* church. "That's the Flintstones!" he said, referring to his own early exposure to tongues as a church camp volunteer where children were being taught (*read*: forced) to speak in this foreign "language" - and engage in this mysterious and unusual behavior.

I may have been too young to care about this spiritual practice. Without understanding the words, I was baffled and fearful, a traumatic throwback to my childhood "Yugy" orthodoxy perhaps, although the latter was not quite so intimidating. I'm reminded now of a scene in the film *The Eyes of Tammy Baker*, where the child-Tammy Faye spews out indecipherable words in church and passes out. Scary!

20

To me, losing control was unnatural and weird, a line I never wanted to cross. Perhaps I should have read Proverbs 3:5-6: "Trust the Lord with all your heart and lean not on your own understanding; in all your ways submit to him, and he will make your paths straight."

Now the word *Pentecost* and concept is less scary because I'm better informed. It's part of the Catholic Church calendar, such as Pentecost Sunday following Easter. But the *-ism* is still a mystery and carries some unfortunate baggage from childhood.

Pop Mother and Child: *Original* 48″ x 34″ (122 x 86 cm)

Pop Mother and Child

Musical Ministry OR "We Were Designed to Sing"

Music (and media) remains a huge influence on my faith, as well as my later unapologetic and fateful return to the Catholic faith. Music of all kinds makes sense of everything; often, where words fail, music speaks. We had to laugh when the lead singer at St. Jude the Apostle Church (not The Beatles "(Hey) Jude") began a song by encouraging the congregation to "Lift up your voices...the *worse* the better!"

Psalm 100 extols us to "Make a joyful noise unto the Lord, all ye lands. Serve the Lord with gladness: come before his presence with singing." Singing is not only a joyful noise (or as Neil Diamond, the "Jewish Elvis" put it: *"a beautiful noise")* but also a way to connect with the meaning and message of the gospel.

Not only in the sanctuary of a church, but musical performance has also spread from the choir to the mainstream stage. Some hit musicals started out as school concerts, such as the enchanting *Joseph and the Amazing Technicolor Dreamcoat.* The 1968 pop cantata written by Andrew Lloyd Webber and Tim Rice for an English school made such an impression that it went on to be recorded as an album. Eventually, after touring the U.S. and U.K. as an amateur production circa 1970s, *Joseph...* became a bona fide Broadway rock musical.

Come-to-Jesus Moments

As far-fetched as it might sound, other hit musicals of that era, namely *Godspell* and *Jesus Christ Superstar,* added to and fired up my understanding and love of God and Jesus. The strong messages and storytelling of those three blockbusters hooked not just me but took Jesus mainstream.

Godspell was a more personal visit with the words of St. Matthew; and intimate right down to sharing wine (representing the blood of Jesus) in a stand-in "church" in the middle of Melbourne: The Playbox Theatre. I loved how *Godspell* cast Jesus and his lot (disciples) as everyday (read non-Biblical) *people.* Instead of glorifying Him - and putting J.C. - on a pedestal.

Watching the show (which seemed like a billion zillion times), I learned the apostles' testaments and the first gospel in the Bible, fueled by having a mad crush on Colleen Hewett (in a nice, not stalker way), who belted

23

out the signature song "Day by Day." I lost count of how many "night by nights" I heard that show-stopping tune; also on the wireless (radio) but each time, oh, how it moved my soul. (I actually managed to meet her after a matinee…and kept ringing her, until her husband put the kibosh on my calls!) I was under the "God spell" of St. Matt and couldn't get enough religion!

On the other hand, *Jesus Christ Superstar* was a spectacular in-your-face experience. The powerful and vivid figures of Jesus (and especially Judas) hit my impressionable younger self hard. Visceral, song after song, plus the powerful driving orchestral score, pounded in my brain as it ran through the audience like an electric current. The Holy Trinity on fire!

A sledgehammer to the soul. What *Superstar* did so brilliantly was to humanize Mary and the Apostles, bringing the Bible to life (*Godspell* with rock!).

The *JCS* production struck a more vivid, deeper chord within me than just reading the Good Book. Undeniably, an unforgettable super-star experience that rocked my world. (I was fortunate enough to witness the incomparable Marcia Hines as Mary Magdalene, the first Black female performer to grace the stage in that role. Another teenage crush: *I knew how to love her!*).

Cut to many moons later…I *met* Jesus! While working backstage as part of the motley crew during a production of *Jesus Christ Superstar*, I had a divine, ethereal vision: Ted Neely, the performer, as Jesus, walking towards me in the wings after a scene—white-gowned, bearded and flowing long hair—smiling beatifically.

"I just saw JESUS!" I crowed to my wife and friends, believers and pagans alike. There were confused looks from most of them, who had no idea how to take my revelation—except for the ones who *got* me. It was both personal and spiritual, a surreal musical epiphany! I was gobsmacked…or should that be Godsmacked?

Flashback to the 1970s musical *Hair.* My first taste of live musical theater at the ripe old age of 15. The eponymous title song with the lyrics "Gimme a head of hair….long as God can grow it, my hair like Jesus wore it, Hallelujah I adore it. Hallelujah Mary loved her son, why don't my mother love me?" Right?

Finally, something contemporary I could relate to! The love I craved and the locks I loved despite the criticism. *"Biblical"* hair was just one of many descriptions in that exciting, irreverent, radical American Tribal Love-Rock Musical that led to my lifelong love of rock musical theater.

On a side note, I'm that geeky guy who reads the program or *Playbill* cover to cover, looking for obscure biblical references in a performer's bio, even when it's not a so-called "spiritual" show. Then, I'll rush home and obsessively look up these references. Take this one in *Buddy: The Buddy Holly Story*. David Reed lists his credits and thanks (to his family and faith...) and ends with Jeremiah 29:11: "For I know the plans I have for you."

Truth be told, I hadn't done that in my own show bios (as a lapsed actor) due to my former lack of scholarship about the Good Book, but I probably will in the future. (*Note to Self:* It's a subtle tribute to our Maker, a way to honor God. And share the *Good word*).

Say Your Prayers

Whereas the above-mentioned musical productions and shows were quite literal, the musical messages of the Lord have usually been more subtle in rather unexpected ways. In Metallica's controversial (inspired by Sudden Infant Death Syndrome- SIDS) heavy metal hit *Enter Sandman,* a sampling of the children's bedtime prayer "Now I lay me down to sleep" creeps in. Most folks mistakenly think of it as scriptural, but it's attributed to a circa 18th-century prayer that includes "I pray the Lord my soul to keep." (I don't know about you, but it always scared the bejeezus out of my friend Shari, when her mother would repeat it to her at bedtime: *"What do you mean if I DIE before I wake?!!"*).

Another interesting bit of trivia is how a pop-rock version of *The Lord's Prayer* became a secular sensation. Recorded by Australian nun Sister Janet Mead, (back in the day) it sold over two million copies !

Even with its overtly religious lyrics—"Our Father Who Art in Heaven, Hallowed Be Thy Name, Thy Kingdom Come, Thy Will Be Done, On Earth as it is in Heaven"—it took the 3rd and 4th positions on top music charts, (selling twice as many copies as Metallica's *Enter Sandman,* which propelled them to mega-star prominence) whilst she appropriately resisted the allure of notoriety. Interestingly, the former music teacher was an early adopter of the *Rock Mass* as a way to make the Lord's message more accessible—which has certainly been attractive to me. Combining Catholic and Christian elements, with sacred and secular texts, set to contemporary musical styles, including rock.

Christ Nailed It

"There's nothing better than a good laugh. I think God gave us a sense of humor because we've got to find a release somehow in the midst of everything else that's going on in our lives," said Fanny Flagg, quoted in a *Unity* magazine article. Fanny nailed it. Humor is super important in any setting, even in a churchy church. How does it serve us to be heavy and laborious? Are we any less serious or committed? Frankly, I think that puts off a lot of people from attending a Sunday service.

I recall a favorite giddy moment from the local Ascension Lutheran church when cheeky Pastor Tim was dispensing communion. His great wit and quick mind made him a comic cleric. Having once heard my Brit colloquial expression "Bob's your uncle," he handed me the wafer and improvised in a stage whisper: "This is the body of Christ shed for you...*Bob*." I nearly choked on the holy host!

Dad loved telling jokes ad nauseam. Don't think it mattered to Pop that I'd cringe when I heard blasphemy, no matter how innocuous. One of his faves was about Paddy, a drunken priest who, weaving through the village, runs into the vicar. The vicar raises an eyebrow disapprovingly: "Drunk again, O'Malley?" "Me too!" responds the inebriated Paddy.

In general, religious jokes make me uncomfortable. To be old school about it, it irks me when people break the 3rd Commandment: *Thou shalt not take the name of the Lord thy God in vain.* Anyway, I inevitably butcher the punchlines. I'll admit though to having a soft spot for the wicked and wise a-la-Eire humor, like this one about the Irishman who is struggling to find a parking space:

"Lord," he prayed, "I can't stand this. If you open a space for me, I swear I'll give up the Guinness and go to mass every Sunday." Suddenly, the clouds part and the sun shines on an empty parking spot (*blaring of heavenly trumpets*). Without hesitation, the Irishman says: "Never mind, I found one!"

"Percy The Postie" (cartoon strip) by Doug Durich

Mass Media

After graduating from college with a B.A. in media studies, my goal was to land a job in electronic media, ideally in radio with the ABC—the *Australian* Broadcasting Corporation. After underemployment, a stack of applications, a plethora of mostly unanswered phone calls and prayer aplenty—my prayers were answered: I was offered my dream job at ABC Radio! (Apparently, God was the late-night DJ who'd taken my request.)

With a multitude of potential departments and programs within the corporation, which position was I serendipitously offered? Albeit temporarily, one in *religious programs*! Was this meant to be? A God nudge? I believed so. Giving glory to God (in the Highest), I was rapt on high.

By the grace of God Almighty, work was mine again. Not exactly as easy as A-B-C, but it did indeed have the stamp of doing God's work. A kind of specialized ministry—and paid at that. Days were spent happily hunched over a Remington typewriter in the confines of a boring business suit, typing passages from the Bible and the parables as well as listening to, recording and editing sacred music. My former laborless despair ended, my days were now significant and purpose-filled. Heaven on Earth!

I believed this was serving Him, not in a lofty or self-righteous way, but pragmatically. A job for Jesus. If I wasn't interested in or didn't have time to read the Word of God before, I was most assuredly afforded this opportunity now. I was steeping in his Word like a tea bag in an all-day cuppa! I do like this corny but clean joke: *How does Moses make tea?? Hebrews it !*

27

Then, God, working in His mysterious ways, seemingly dropped the next gig onto my résumé: as a PR guy with Fusion Australia, working on, amongst other campaigns (*drum roll please*): the Easter '93 Christian marches in Sydney and Melbourne (*ba dum...tsss)*!...bringing God to the streets. The charismatic Mal Garvin was the head honcho of the media conglomerate that included Christian radio broadcasting. I was drawn to Fusion because it was God-based and had a universal message as well as an international outreach. Also its radio ministry. Praying was not only encouraged but embraced and orchestrated into our workday. Alas, faith-wise, I was thrown for a bit of a loop when Garvin scandalously fell from grace.

What's all of this got to do with the big-C Catholicism? Zippo. Nada. Nothing perhaps. I do however firmly believe we have to sample what there is in the grand smörgåsbord of life until we find what we like—or love—spiritually and then go back for second helpings. And I happen to love Roman Catholicism, especially with its mystery and reverence of the Holy Father and the Saints, Mother Mary and her Son Jesus.

Even the Pope – *Papa*- has a certain inexpicable draw, perhaps fascination- with his message of love, despite the controversial public perceptions of him (and previous Pontiffs). And his being a father figure... Something I need -as do others, I believe.

© Joe Heller, 2013

II. WANDERING

"I search for God and found only myself. I search for myself and find only God."

–Rumi

From Apple to Angels

After a brief infatuation with the Big Apple, New York City, I vowed to return to "Our Lady the Queen of the Angels"—better known as Los Angeles—after stopping there en route to Melbourne in the early 1980s. With that in mind, a few years later, I signed up for a Writers Tour starting in San Francisco and culminating with the Santa Barbara Writers Conference. On our heady itinerary, I was drawn to the literary scene in the City-by-the-Bay, especially the indie bookstores and famed Beat Generation writers (such as Jack Kerouac, Allen Ginsberg and William S. (*Naked Lunch*) Burroughs.

Heading down the Pacific Coast on our tour bus was fascinating, not only for the hand of God in its breathtaking scenery but also for the Franciscan missions that form the 600-mile El Camino Real. A total of nine of its twenty-one missions were founded by Franciscan missionary Fr. Junipero Serra, hence, the Serra Retreat that inaugurated this book.

Santa Barbara and its environs appropriately are dubbed the American Riviera; although since that first viewing of its grand mission, I've always thought of it as Heaven on Earth. Auspiciously, I met my future wife, Kitty, at that 1991 Writers Conference in Montecito, Santa Barbara . I proposed and tied the knot in the autumn- "Fall" - of 1993 in Thousand Oaks.

"It's a Nice Day for a White Wedding"

If, as Billy Idol sings, "there's nothin' sure in this world," then neither Kitty nor I should have been surprised by our unusual wedding. Maybe it was reflective of the multiplicity of most things in my complex life. The originally scheduled Science of Mind minister for our Lutheran church ceremony turned out to be a "disappointing 'no-show'" (in the words of my soon-to-be brother-in-law, Mike) and was replaced by a last-minute Lutheran officiant Kitty knew. Too bad her twin, Kathy, hadn't yet been ordained, to do the honors.

30

That would have been a meaningful moment and an extra-special spiritual and family memory.

Outlaws

Kitty's family turned out to be more spiritual than religious—not necessarily subscribers to organized religion or presenting as traditional believers—but rather in mysterious, subterranean ways in contrast to mine, which could hardly be described as "spiritual." Certainly not radical nor even pleasantly mellow, my family was mainstream, traditional and conservative in their walk- and talk (*read*: rigid). As diverse as the differences between Hare Krishnas and Catholics.

Elissa, the "Urban Shaman"

In the younger generation, we have an Urban Shaman amongst the branches of our non-Native American family tree. Elissa (daughter of Kitty's twin, Kathy) follows Native American traditional beliefs, being in harmony with Nature—the elements of the Sun, Wind, Fire and Water—and the Great Spirit, the concept of a life force or Supreme Being.

The unconventional Lisse is an Old Soul. Raised by both Kitty and Kathy, the proverbial apple didn't fall far from the tree. Like her mother and aunt, she's a free spirit who thinks deeply and is advanced in her beliefs.

"I identified as pagan, then a friend introduced me to becoming a Shaman. I don't think of myself as being religious but as spiritual." When I asked what she thought of traditional organized religion, our niece forthrightly responded: "a rigorous practice immediately comes to mind." As much as I understand her—or as you, Dear Reader, by now have surmised–I respect her and others' views of organized religion. Summarizing, she says: "I think more in terms of a *belief* system. I'm a *modern* Shaman."

I find it interesting that she follows a metaphysical faith and is of a generation who doesn't feel it necessary to belong to a church, yet they still believe in something greater than themselves.

Mystic in a Business Suit

My American brother-in-law, Mike, studied comparative religion and managed to meet the Dalai Lama. I was equally impressed *and* green with envy. What's the traditional Buddhist perspective on that latter unwholesome emotion? It made Buddha's list of defilements of the mind, along with hypocrisy, fraud, and arrogance!

As told to me, here are his impressions about this brief but auspicious meeting:

> *Around 1983...I'd already been meditating for about 11 years and had professional roles as a fundraising executive. Although I'd quietly become a closet mystic in a business suit, very few knew about my mystical experiences. I came to sit with His Holiness in the Newport Beach Country Club meeting room.* However, as Kundan's dialogue unfolded (a form of address for the Dalai Lama, meaning presence), *I realized there was exactly nothing a Westerner with such a mind-frame could ask him that anyone hadn't already asked him before. When H.H. was done addressing our audience on kindness, compassion, joy and peace, there was applause...after which everyone left very quickly. I sat very deferentially for him...he rose from his chair, and I followed his lead. He noticed my intentions and walked up to me and bowed. I reciprocated...and then we left.* (*The Shamanic Powers of Rolling Thunder*, 2016, Anthology)

Mike is adamant that *Autobiography of a Yogi* by Paramahansa Yogananda changed his life. "Yogananda, Yukteswar and Mahasaya are teaching me things and confirming things I never expected but dearly needed." (Or perhaps it was the articulate audiobook narration by the actor Ben Kingsley that he found so compelling?).

My religion is very simple
My religion is kindness
- Dalai Lama

Kathy

My late sister-in-law, Kathy (Kitty's identical twin) also embodied the family trait of duality. She was an ordained Science of Mind (SOM aka Church of Religious Science) minister who, despite her traditional Presbyterian upbringing, was also metaphysical. Committed to the New Thought faith of Ernest Holmes and its teachings, Kathy embraced its philosophy: (a) the belief in the unity of all life; (b) that intentions flow through consciousness; and (c) to honor and accept all faiths, including Christianity (with which I also resonate).

And So It Is. The SOM faithful substitute this invocation for *Amen* after prayer to bless their intentions into being. With a nod to Pascal–or perhaps out of nostalgia–I offer both respectfully after praying without risking aspersions from the broad-minded "all-in-God" panentheistic believers.

Putting aside our differences–or perhaps to mollify Kitty–my intense but now dearly departed Seattle sister-in-law seemed to tolerate my live-and-let-live ethos and unconventional, freewheeling ways. I like to think that she respected my open nature and bohemian artistry, as she accepted me into the tight-knit fold of dem Dills as the first foreigner from an eclectic spiritual background. (Kathy, may you Rest In Peace —but I finally get the last word!) .

Last but not Louisest

Louise Lorenz was my late mother-in-law. Speaking of free spirits, I'm certain this glamorous blonde dame was a non-practicing (or, at the very least, latent) Catholic; unchurched as far as we know. Her eclectic apartment draped with rosary beads, scapular, carved crosses and other depictions of Mary, and Catholic relics may have been more than just pretty things such as the beautiful antique Bible and colorful worry beads discovered after her passing. I believe this creative soul was not only an unrecognized artist but also a Sister of Jesus. A kind of *Catholic-in-Law.* However, her son Mike, bless him, was convinced she was under the influence of the more culturally fervent circles in which she ardently moved. Even if I didn't agree with him, she was indeed gullible but also altruistic with fellow humans or especially critters.

I never take off the St. Christopher medal that she gave me. AKA the "Saint of Travel," no longer just for ambitious travel does it shine; its protection accompanies me in my jaunts around the City of a Thousand Malls.

Apparently, Louise liked to travel too. I'd like to have borrowed the T-shirt she wore irreverently to our wedding: "London. Paris. New York. Thousand Oaks."

"For we are God's handiwork, created in Christ Jesus to do good works, which God prepared in advance for us to do." Ephesians 2:10

MiseRecordia

My first job in America was at our local, eclectic Tower Records working with a bunch of bohemian misfits who turned out to be rather cool characters. I never confided my Christianity at work nor, for that matter, anywhere except at church and with trusted people. After a few months of music dealing, out of the blue, a colleague whispered to me conspiratorially: "Are you a Christian?" Exposed, I was taken aback and acknowledged I was. He, pierced and tattooed, smiled and responded: "So am I!" He'd sensed something about me, but I'd never suspected I was working with a fellow "fisherman," a brother in Christ. It was our little secret.

Then, in 1994, I was offered a job in Hollywood at Applied Scholastics, the Church of Scientology's offshoot educational arm where I'd worked part-time in Sydney. It was flattering but not feasible; at that point, it was too controversial despite its much-cloaked affiliation with Scientology.

Not to Be Confused with...

Fortunately, courtesy of my newly wedded spouse, I found myself working in the office of the Church of Religious Science, aka Science of Mind, in Thousand Oaks. A church we belonged to, she loved and I warmed to, although it seemed rather far out and American compared to the staid churches of my youth.

Beverly—the office manager with a Texas twang—and little ol' me—with my "What part-of-England-are-you-from?" accent—made quite an odd team. But it was good for the résumé and closer and safer than crazy Holly*weird,* even though my mother-in-law, Angie, considered the church a cult and naively confused it with the Church of Scientology. She was certainly not the only cuddly toy... My parents shared the same fear. That I'd be drawn into some weird American sect, certainly a doctrine different from Mum's European Orthodox one.

Science of Mind, or New Thought, undoubtedly was a new mindset for me. For instance, the law of cause and effect, where thoughts are things:

every thought creates either by adding to or detracting from this energy. I felt more self-confident and able to express love more freely. At least I was making an honest living and could walk to work while learning about this spiritual-metaphysical religion.

If you believe *everything* is sacred as I do, you may subscribe to Carl Jung's beautiful summation "Despite all our differences, the unity of mankind will assert itself irresistibly." Amen! *And So It Is!*

A God Job

Though it may not always feel like it, our jobs or any paid work can be a blessing. "Our work allows us to utilize God-given talents and to grow personally and professionally," according to an *In Touch* magazine Sunday Reflection. My wife is fond of telling people I have a "God job." Our work is not just our job, but our gift to God and those we work for or with. I comfort myself with this thought after a difficult day or when I'm feeling underappreciated.

God does not require that we be successful, only that we be faithful. God calls on us to cooperate. "The God who made the world and everything in it does not live in temples made by man, nor is he served by human hands, as though he needed anything, since he himself gives to all mankind life and breath and everything" (Acts 17:24–25)

Passport to Massports

According to an article in *Peer* Magazine, the first 300 years of the Church were its most formative. My early reverence for churches, pews, priests, pastors and altars and all that atmosphere later led me to explore those first 300-plus years by visiting churches and chapels throughout Europe and the U.S.

Mind-blowing St. Peter's Basilica and the incomparable neck-cricking Sistine Chapel. Gladly glared down upon by gruesome Gothic gargoyles atop the magnificent Notre Dame.

Westminster Abbey, officially called the Royal Peculiar, the posh last London address of the holy and the infamous. Adjacent St. Margaret's, the unofficial parish church of the House of Commons and site of Winston Churchill's 1908 wedding is where commoners Kitty and Gordon Durich renewed their wedding vows in 1998.

Kitty and I visited stunning churches throughout Europe, including Vienna's most significant cathedral, St. Stephen's. In 2013, we attended a special service at a unique sacral building in Podgorica, capital city of Montenegro (where I have ancestral roots). The Cathedral Church of Christ's Resurrection was consecrated Catholically on the jubilee marking the issuance of the Edict of Milan—a proclamation of religious tolerance for Roman-era Christians 1,700 years before!

The most famous church in New York City is no doubt the neo-Gothic revival St. Patrick's Cathedral (*St. Patty's* to nonchalant locals) on fashionable 5th Avenue in Manhattan. In stark contrast, the Bowery Mission serves the homeless and marginalized on the Lower East Side, both New York City treasures. Also, there's the grand Times Square church, where I joined fellow worshipers from over 100 nationalities. I try to attend a service at one church in every city I visit, especially in my "second home" of NYC. I love the contrasts of these places of worship and people.

One special Christmas memory is the especially warm welcome I received at the Nineteenth Street Baptist Church, considered the first Black Baptist congregation in Washington, D.C. Founded in 1839, it felt inclusively Christian to be the only Caucasian participant at that historic congregation—familiar and comforting with a twist of soul-stirring gospel music!

It's great to experience community with people who love Jesus and feel at home and mesh spiritually whether it's in Melbourne, Malibu or Manhattan.

Church of the Open Mind

I'd met Kitty at the 1991 Santa Barbara Writers Conference before moving to the U.S. in 1993. During that interlude, my wife-to-be introduced me to Science of Mind. Also known as (Church of) Religious Science, its simple, universal philosophy is *God is within you.*

Conceptualized in the 20th century by Ernest Holmes as a humanistic, metaphysical model, it was a radical departure from the punitive, fear-based teachings of the traditional Bible-based churches in which I was raised. I loved its open-minded ways, and it's still part of our repertoire, with charismatic pastors such as the earnest and warm Rev. Sue and the theatrically based, yet deep, Dr. James.

God is the One. The One power and the power of Love. I believe God comes first, like our Heavenly Father, who gave us life, and eternal life at that. I used to believe He was above us on a white cloud. That's probably when I

36

believed the Tooth Fairy left a penny under my pillow or the Easter Bunny brought a basketful of eggs. How did that add up? We need to somehow appease ourselves even if it is sometimes delusional!

"It's not atheism that's destroying religion, it's religion,"

Phillip Adams, Australian broadcaster

Panspirituality and Pascal

So, can a case be made for being panspiritual: believing in and belonging to a myriad of faiths, from Christianity to Confucianism? Is it fear of missing out (*FOMO*) that attracts some people (including yours truly) to attend multiple churches? I know a couple–she's Catholic and he's Lutheran–who compromise by doing rotations (without conflict) on alternate Sundays to a Catholic mass and a Lutheran service. Sometimes, Kitty and I attend two churches in the same morning, equally connected to both without feeling we're double-dipping or diluting their messages.

The 17th-century French philosopher and mathematician Blaise Pascal pragmatically played the odds in the debate of believing-not believing in God:

"If God exists and I believe in God, I'll go to heaven, which is infinitely good. If God exists and I don't believe in God, I may go to hell, which is infinitely bad. If God does not exist, then whether I believe in God or not, whatever I'd gain or lose would be finite. So, I should believe in God."

The Many-Gods Objection was the rebuttal to Pascal's wager, mainly: There are many religions, and believing in the God of one religion might prevent gaining the infinite rewards of another religion. Eckhart Tolle's definition, in his seminal *A New Earth,* seems more in line with both Pascal's and my own experiences: perhaps modality–the channel–is less important than "the underlying energy-frequency that flows into what you do."

"For What It's Worth" (Stephen Stills)

As the sharply perceptive and not merely poetic Lennon said: "God is not an old man in the sky…God is something in all of us." Nor was he, as my Jewish friend once believed, the white-clad Sunshine baker on the boxes

37

of her childhood cookies. God is also not in you like "a raisin in the roll," as Unity Minister Eric Butterworth (not Mrs. Butterworth's) wrote in his *The Mystery of God in Man,* but "like the ocean is in a wave." I love the power of that Universal All-ness.

Spreading Butterworth's wisdom (the cleric's not the syrup), let's continue along the edible theme as Psalm 34:8 tempts us with: "Taste and see that the Lord is good. Happy are those who take refuge in Him." That's how I perceive God: As a savior. After all, there's only one letter difference between *savior* and *savor.* Not everyone has the same leanings, whether towards food or towards faith (the latter, if at all). "The more we pursue Him, the greater our craving will be." Isn't that the way it goes? A wayward seed we unconsciously plant that grows into a tree bearing fruit. *Amen!*

"Two Tickets to Paradise" (Eddie Money)

A scene in the movie *We Own the Night* highlights this paradox. One character observes another: "You're wearing a Jewish star *and* a cross…are you confused?" Like that character, I was not confused. But I do wear a St. Christopher medal around my neck, Buddhist *mala* beads on my wrist and, hidden in my pocket, a small wooden cross (given to me by a lay minister).

Then there's the opposite: a rejection of Christianity—remote and foreign to me.

"Christianity in America is in a decline despite America boasting it's a Christian nation," says Charles Coulter, founder and pastor of Church at Home. "More and more Christians are saying the Church is irrelevant to the issues of real life." People are leaving the more traditional churches—and, indeed, Christianity—in droves yet flocking to centers of belief like Atmosphere, my Christian non-denominational church *du jour.* According to its pastor, Jim Crews, "Church is not an event; it's a lifestyle."

Some sources point out that church attendance is declining. Becoming untethered to any organized religion is, to put it crudely, being like a dog without a bone; in high-brow terms, it's a loss of theological deliverance from harm and a secular separation of church and state. Freedom of belief and the "spiritual but not religious/affiliated" or "more spiritual than religious" movement has no doubt had a part to play. However, a recent NPR story commented that post-Covid church attendance has increased, although more clergy are leaving due to burnout.

In my opinion, it's *all* good and perceived as positive as long as you *believe* in a Higher Power—whatever that means to *you*—and stay open-minded. That's the bottom line, right? *Allah, God, Yahweh, Nyame, the King of Kings, Krishna, Hu, Rama, Mulungu, Brahman, Olorun, Parusha, the Supreme Self, Ogun, even the Universal Mother.* Or reality TV's Annie Suwan's characteristic exclamation: "Oh, my Buddha!" Sometimes we have to stop trying to name names and just let go and let God.

Meant to Be

Out of the blue often comes inexplicable cravings for something comforting, much like a cooling swirl of a strawberry frozen yogurt on a hot summer's "arvo" (Australian for afternoon) or porridge (Oz for oatmeal) for a perfect winter brekky. I didn't just wake up one morning, snap my fingers, and believe in God. "Hmm, I think I'll be a Roman Catholic today and count some rosary beads." Voila! Maybe I'll be a Buddhist monk!" No motives or need for inclusion or attention: it is I firmly believe, a calling from the omnipresent and eternal God. In Proverbs 3:5-6 it says not to rely on our *own* understanding but to "trust the Lord, with all our hearts.

Ah, Elusive Faith!

"Faith is believing in something you can't explain." This text from my insomniac Jewish friend dropped the mic at the ungodly hour of 1 a.m. when she'd heard it on a late-night radio talk show. Similarly, Elizabeth Gilbert, in her bestselling memoir *Eat, Pray, Love* wrote: "Faith is belief in what you cannot see or prove."

Consider this reassuring contribution from the Book of Matthew (21:22 ESV): "And whatever you ask in prayer, you will receive, if you have *faith*." These statements contribute to unresolved devotion to the Almighty; especially, in my opinion, praying. "If you do not stand firm in your faith," it says in Isaiah 7:9, "you will not stand at all." (Perhaps Alexander Hamilton was inspired by Isaiah?)

Faith and Hope, not Infamy

I'd heard about the book *Faith, Hope and Carnage*–a conversational dialogue between Nick Cave and Sean O'Hagan–from Flea, the bass player for the über-successful Red Hot Chili Peppers. Melbourne-born Flea has always been on my radar as a musician and author, so I had to check it out. Nick Cave, another Aussie, is an intriguing songwriter and singer I've followed since the 1970s. We share the same birth year and I once had the opportunity to work with him in Melbourne before we were famous. Correction: *He* was and still is. (*Does that make me infamous?*)

Cave is a lapsed Anglican. He was reared in the faith but distanced himself from God and organized religion at age 19 after his father's death. "Remote, alien and uncertain," is how he saw God. And I get it even though I do not share that view of God. To me, God is more personal, ethereal and certain. I think as we get older, we either mellow with age or, unfortunately for some, become more bitter.

In the chapter, "The Utility of Belief," Cave headbutts faith with surprising statements like, "Religion is spirituality with rigor…for me, it involves some wrestling with the idea of faith—that seam of doubt that runs through most credible religions. It's the struggle with the notion of the divine that is at the heart of my creativity."

In Cave's case, I think time has unified his faith and music, which he describes in the book as the "God-bothering" religious shows he performed with his first band, The Birthday Party. "With all that rolling around on stage and purging demons and speaking in tongues…I was always trying to find some kind of spiritual home."

Religio-Catechesis
At some point, I was struck by the realization that I'd sampled the alphabet soup of organized mainstream religions looking for my spiritual home: Anglican, Baptist, Buddhist, Catholic, Church of England, Hindu, Lutheran, Methodist, Orthodox plural and Presbyterian. Even the "exotic" taste of Judaism. Islam, I have yet to experience—and the LDS Church, or Mormons, if they'll have me.

However, propelled by my curiosity, I still hadn't settled on the right "flavor," as a flippant friend once chided me skeptically. The mature perspective is that it's not as much about the *building*, one's holy place; it's about being aware, exploring and following one's heart along with the belief that God is calling. We just need to answer.

"Jesus came to disturb the comfortable and comfort the disturbed."
-Heard at Bible Study

Still Searching

If you're feeling frazzled by so many directions to turn to and not knowing where or how to worship, conservative or contemporary, you're not alone. There are multiple places of worship to choose from and a wide spectrum of theology.

I believe God nudges us in our hearts to act. Like writing this book, a journey, a self-struggle, facing personal demons. A steady drumbeat of faith—from empty childhood churches to golf course alternative sanctuaries—a process of unapologetic and unbridled credulity.

III. FOUND

"I once was lost but now I'm found."

-Amazing Grace,
Christian hymn

Of Boxes, Birds and Buddhists

Fast-forward: I'd followed my (religion) to California in the US of A—yet still begged the question: How could I stave off my insatiable curiosity when my mind's like a magnet and every little thing seems to pluck a resonant chord? Ugh! Being plagued with a curious mind can lead one down rabbit holes and open up way too many a Pandora's Box!

A fellow artist and believer at Snapdragon Healing Arts Center (where I was an Artist *sans* Residence at this charming yellow cottage of art + spirituality) teasingly called me a magpie: "Always collecting bits and bobs of useless objects and information." *(Cheeky magpies are also known for their bold personality and intellect!)*

Don't Just Do Something, Sit There!

I remember a friend arriving at my art show reception with her British friend in tow. "Hi, I'm Sonya and I'm a Buddhist," she announced. The confidence she exuded along with her blatant pronouncement intrigued introverted me. I had to know more!

Buddha taught that happiness comes from inner peace rather than external conditions. Without inner peace, outer peace is impossible. To progress along a spiritual path to attain inner peace and eventually full enlightenment, Buddhists engage in regular practices of meditation and daily activities such as chanting *Nam Myoho Renge Kyo* (sound familiar?).

The meditative state of *being* was soothing, almost hypnotic, and transformative. Buddhahood's "Enlightenment" and "suffering-is-optional" thinking may have made perfect sense; however, as a meditation or lifestyle, it was not enough to satisfy me nor sustain the true worship of God that was coursing bone-deep in my veins.

"You deserve your own love and affection," affirms the Buddhist magazine *Lion's Roar*. I understood that chanting was meant to connect me to my Buddha nature—but mine apparently had ADHD and had left the room!

42

Chanting *Nam Myoho Renge Kyo* over and over was too repetitive, too predictable and (sorry) too boring!

Monk in a Mall

The tranquility of suburbia is occasionally transformed with energetic enterprise. In the heart of Ventura County, California, the Kadampa Meditation Center introduced Buddhist meditation to the masses at—of all places—the Thousand Oaks shopping mall. *(Maybe it should be rechristened "The City of a Thousand Malls"?)*

Founder of 1,000 Kadampa Meditation Centers worldwide, Western Buddhist Monk Geshe Kelsang Gyatso was ordained a Buddhist monk at the tender age of 8. (And what was I doing at that tender age besides grubbing for tadpoles?) He teaches at Tushita Kadampa Buddhist Center inside The Oaks, the local upscale busy mall.

I went to a free meditation at The Oaks one Saturday evening, where he was appearing for an evening of enlightenment that turned out to be filled with much insight and humor. I expected only a handful of people to show up. After all, this was a Saturday evening in a suburban mall with a Macy's and a food court, and not exactly Malibu. Surprisingly, nearly a hundred people were there! Macy's shoppers wandering over? Close proximity to that coffee and Chinese food? Or maybe locals looking for enlightenment in unlikely places?

"Buddha Nature" (Pen & Ink) by the Author

Finding My Religion (a nod and wink to R.E.M.)
"A church is not a building; a church is its people."
　　　　　　　　　　Pastor Jim Crews, Atmosphere Church

Nowadays, you will find me attending my newest auxiliary faith home, Atmosphere. I discovered it as a non-denominational church that originally "teed off" its Sunday service at a golf course, alternating between outdoor services in a lush amphitheater and the indoor comfort of a cozy ballroom. While Atmosphere is my prayer place, Global Truth Center-LA is my meditation spot: A balance and, like most matters in my life, a positive dichotomy—from faith to autonomy.

Embracing your spirituality doesn't have to be about religion. It means accepting that you have value and your life matters. Author Gregory Scott Brown, MD, said: "I love to ask my patients: 'What do you think about spirituality?' because it almost always leads to deeper discussions about connection, purpose and the meaning of life."

According to sci-fi writer Douglas Adams, the meaning of life is 42. Huh? With a Pascalian twist, the conundrum that there is an answer as well as it's impossible to know the answer might both be absurd suppositions. The point is asking the right question. What questions should I have asked—or do you need to ask—to find out what is spiritually meaningful?

Several publications I read regularly concur with this article on Delicious Living.com: "7 Dimensions of Active Aging"—and Dr. Brown; namely, that being "spiritual" is an important component or measure of a meaningful life along with the importance of living your "true purpose." Finding where you belong, just as Boy Gordo did.

"It is the heart that feels God, not reason. This is what faith is. God felt by the heart, not by reason." –Blaise Pascal

When the Church Meets the Heart

Pastor Jim of Atmosphere points out that the word *heart* is mentioned 1,000 times in the Bible. Our faith connects us to people, heart-to-heart, who search for more meaning in their lives, and whether or not they know it, they add to our lives spiritually and in myriad other ways.

Devotion

Nina is a very devout Catholic who you might say is in love with the church. Her devotion has always inspired me. "It's my life," she shared.

Even when it comes to something as significant as worship. For someone like Nina, attending twice a year is not nearly enough. "I've been a Byzantine Greek Ukrainian Catholic for 70 years. I attend daily Mass. It's a wedding feast: the Holy Eucharist is the consummation of the bride (us) and the groom (Christ). It is the highest form of divine worship! Being Saints."

Two Loves

Seth shares profoundly: "I was baptized and confirmed in the Lutheran Church when I met my wife, Barbara. I was very devoted to Christ and to seeking the truth, but I was not a member of any church. She told me she was Catholic, and I immediately asked if she would take me to a Catholic Church service. It turned out to be our first date. I fell in love twice that day: with Barbara *and* the Mass." I so love this story.

Special Souls

At my bread-and-butter job, when I work with special abilities (formerly known as special needs) souls, I've experienced a couple of Catholic clients who couldn't be more different from each other.

Evan, who was devout and churchgoing under the influence of his parents, religiously wore (when reminded) a saint on a chain around his neck and was prayer-aware. Ken was an unchurched "Chreaster" (attending Christmas and Easter masses), or "C.E.O." (Christmas and Easter Only, in the words of Pastor Jim) mostly with my encouragement. "I come from a 'peaceful religion' family," by which he means "ways of peace that are positive, not apocalyptic, happy and friendly, with no war."

When breaking bread (actually, pizza) with a current high-functioning, open-hearted client, I make a habit of saying grace quite pointedly before our meals. At first, he looks a bit confused; then right on cue, he chimes in: *Amen!* I wouldn't witness him, but I'd gleefully oblige if he asks questions about God and church. I once had a client who requested that I take him to Sunday morning mass as part of my job duties. Thank you, God!

What's Up, Doc?

On my first visit, my new doctor asked me what this book was about. I told him and, with a satisfied smile, he handed me an old-school Patient

Information handout. As directed, I looked at the back side of his mission statement-cum-manifesto. Following "avoid alcohol and smoking" and "decrease stress and take your meds" was "Spirituality." *Check.* "It's very much ignored," Dr. L. said.

When I asked him about his church, he answered (as if it were a Facebook status) "It's complicated." Laughing, I told him I could relate. He confessed he'd gone from Lutheran to Episcopal—and even attended the Church of Religious Science with his former wife. It amazed me how in synch we were. I wasn't the only spiritual goofball, as PJ (Pastor Jim) joked good-naturedly, with a spectrum of beliefs fanning the flames of faith from Bible-based churches that stir my soul to other spiritual "homes."

The Word

The Bible is Moses' book when it comes to the sacred word about God and His people. Spiritual principles change, and generations and teachings express them in contemporary and contextual ways. Indeed, for some, being spiritual is an expression of their transcendent feeling of being at one with nature. One of the most influential Christian leaders of the 20th century, the evangelist Rev. Billy Graham once said: "I believe there are other ways of recognizing the existence of God. Through nature for instance and plenty of other opportunities, therefore in saying 'yes' to God."

"Christo Vero Regi" (Christ is the True King)

Closet Catholic

I identify as a born-again *again* Christian based on Jesus' response in John 3 3:5: "Very truly I tell you, no one can see the kingdom of God unless they are born again from above...no one can enter the kingdom of God without being born of water and the Spirit." My first baptism, (which I don't even remember) was, upon reflection, empty of my accordance and not at all my notion. I was too young and browbeaten.

Being baptized with the Word and the water is akin to dying and being reborn in Christ. The only *visible* way to tell our counter-culture faith is on Ash Wednesday when we fast and are blessed with a crude cross made from ash drawn on our foreheads. I often forget to remove it and get some interesting looks from non-believers!

The other meaningful but subtle way I express my faith is by wearing a St. Christopher medal in place of a ubiquitous cross. I am indeed very much a St. Christopher acolyte. However, if push came to shove, I must *confess* that my absolute favorite Saint would *have* to be that rock star, Saint Francis of Assisi.

An animal lover (and musical to boot), would he have approved that my future-mother-in-law, Louise, smuggled her chihuahua into our wedding in her handbag? His Prayer of St. Francis is my second-favorite prayer (*after* The Serenity Prayer, Psalm 91, which inspired me to create a signature piece of artwork consisting of countless tiny peace signs in the shape of a guitar.

"Lord, make me an instrument of your peace: where there is hatred, let me sow love; where there is injury, pardon; where there is doubt, faith; where there is despair, hope; where there is darkness, light; where there is sadness, joy."

St. Francis of Assisi

Nun-Such

Perhaps artistically and spiritually, you might consider me a hybrid à la Corita Kent aka Sister Corita. We're both worshipers and artists. Kent was a groundbreaking artist who came to prominence in Los Angeles; however, she came from a staunchly religious family and had first been a nun. (No worries; I have no such proclivity.) Her 1960s-era pop art was provocative, incorporating biblical messages such as "Guard Me Oh Lord... As the Apple of My Eye" (*Song with An Apple*, poster, circa 1968). I could relate to her both religiously and artistically. To me, she was like a female version of Andy Warhol.

Other influences on my journey came by way of Colleen, a friend who was a cradle Catholic with a memorable mother. Kaye was not only a terrific English teacher but she was wickedly funny! "There was a nun in my swimming pool when I got home from school today," she'd mention casually. The image of a nun swimming in her full elaborate habit reminded me of a childish proclivity to call them "penguins" (with a modicum of respect of course). We were naughty but nice.

Kaye's offhand comments remind me of my Mum. One time, my sister was going out somewhere special wearing a smart black-and-white ensemble. "You look like a nun," remarked my mother innocently. I laughed out loud but my sister was not amused. To me though, her garb was more elegant than penitent.

From the get-go, I've always held an inexplicable soft spot for nuns. Maybe it came from watching Sally Field as Sister Bertrille in "The Flying Nun" as a kid. Why the affinity for nuns? They represent mystery, grace and pride in wearing their habits in public—in a word, *commitment* to God.

The story goes that Mother Teresa once was assigned a rather grumpy nun; regardless, she still smiled at the dour woman in her sweet, saintly way. One day, perplexed, the nun turned to Mother Teresa and demanded impatiently: "What *is it* you love about me?" The Mother Superior just smiled. The point? God said to *love everyone*, not just *like* them. Mother Teresa had that down pat.

> *"I am a pencil in the hand of God."*
> *Mother/Saint Teresa*

Whenever I notice a nun in public, I never hesitate to say "Hello, Sister." They usually return a surprised smile. Maybe they think I'm weird (*Oh, see Mother Teresa above!*). Probably not many address a woman of the cloth so directly; perhaps they feel intimidated. I do not. I'm not the shy schoolboy I once was—besides, they can no longer whip out a ruler and punish me!

Not too long ago, I participated in the local charity Nun Run (*To Heaven on Foot*) at La Reina High School, a Catholic college prep for girls in Thousand Oaks. I had this image of nuns in habits running in their sneakers, something like the movie *Nuns on the Run*, a British comedy starring one of my favorite comic actors, the brilliant Eric Idle (of *Monty Python's Flying Circus* fame).

Instead, it was mostly the Catholic community coming together and only one sister to say *Good morning* to—and she wasn't wearing sneakers! But I got a shiny medal (my first ever for running—more like staggering—around a couple of city blocks in the City of a Thousand Malls) as well as a fancy Nun Run T-shirt for my efforts. Since I helped sponsor the event, having "Mateship Media" printed on the back of the T-shirt was special.

As the saying goes: "God helps those who help themselves." (Although widely identified as scriptural, apparently, it's not; but it is very old advice.) Consider Deuteronomy 28:8 NIV: *"The Lord will send a blessing on your barns and on everything you put your hand to."*

"Intertwined" by John Conley

Copyright © Brenton 2023

Spiritual Liberation

It says in 2 Corinthians 9:10: "Now he who supplies seed to the sower and bread for food will also supply and increase your store of seed and will enlarge the harvest of your righteousness." Reassuring, and comforting. Trusting in God is easy when life is running smoothly. Heaven knows, it's when we are "hungry," during the hard times in our mortal lives, when we need Him most.

Our faithfulness to Him is maybe not so much the case with conflicting emotions, peer pressures, doubt and the like when our faith and devotion are being tested. I like how Agape founder Rev. Michael Beckwith defines spiritual liberation: "...becoming free from the narrow confines of fear, doubt, worry, and lack, and living instead from a conscious awareness of one's Authentic Self, one's true nature of wholeness."

In Paul's letter to the Philippians, he said: "Have no anxiety about anything, but in everything by prayer and supplication with thanksgiving let your requests be known to God." In a more proactive way, "God helps those who help themselves."

"I don't think that faith, whatever you're being faithful about, really can be scientifically explained. And I don't want to explain this whole life business through truth, science. There's so much mystery. There's so much awe."

-Jane Goodall

The Starry Night

I am not anti-science; and, in spite of being a "closet" Catholic, I'm more spiritual than religious. In comparison, dear old Dad was squarely a science guy. However, Dad might have been wooed by this profound sentiment expressed by the father of my fave *Saturday Night Live* alum, Molly Shannon, in her memoir *Hello, Molly!* "God is the light." And that is how I see Him–or Her–too. I do see God as loving, bright and beautiful.

As Van Gogh said: "God is Nature and Nature is Beauty." How could you not shed a wee tear at this exquisite passage? Shortly before his demise, James Shannon—a lapsed Catholic and an alcoholic (a Catho-holic!) who had caused a family tragedy—scribed this on a yellow legal pad:

> "God is love. God is nature. God is the sun, the moon and the stars and all the planets and the outer universe. God is more than our feeble brain could ever conceive...."

Perhaps, reflecting at the end of their lives, both my Dad and Van Gogh would feel comfortable agreeing with Molly's father. In *Vincent*, (also known as *Starry, Starry Night)* these transcendent lyrics about the artist by troubadour Don McLean struck a chord with me...how Christ-like they sound:

"Now I understand....how you tried to set them free..."

Still Searching

Though I feel I'm closer now than ever, I'll update this story of my sojourn by quoting a U2 song. These immortal words of the inimitable Bono quite likely could be my personal anthem: *"But I still haven't found what I'm looking for...."*

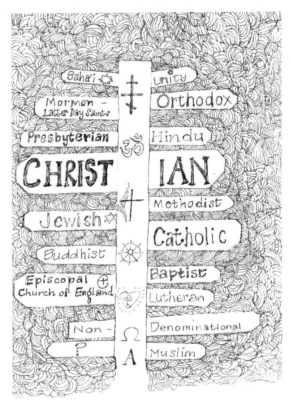

"Signpost" by the Author

Saint Francis of Assisi
"I was sick and you visited me." Matthew 25:36.

In some kind of "poetic justice," for want of a better term, and not meaning to diminish its significance by any means, in that perhaps it was "meant to be," my mother spent her last bittersweet days in palliative care at a Catholic hospice. (Saint Francis Xavier Cabrini, in Melbourne, named after the patron saint of immigrants, Frances Xavier Cabrini).

There, she was given comfort and peace in a beautiful home like setting, to rest. Tranquil, and supportive, with a chapel, where I purchased a small card, that read "Dear Saint Frances, I find myself now in the light of your vision and faith. Turn your loving face towards me and embrace the concerns I carry. Surround me with the peace that you found in the Sacred Heart of Jesus......Amen."

Ironically or not, Cabrini was across the road from family friend, Colleen aforementioned. No coincidence, I believe. And the fact that it was a named after an Italian American Roman Catholic nun, also called "Mother Cabrini." A "God story"? Mum talked about fate. What can you say? Other than God really does work in mysterious ways.

"Remember Him Regularly," Eucharist/Communion comment by Pastor Jim, Atmosphere Church.

"I relax and cast aside all mental burdens, allowing God to express through me His perfect love, peace and wisdom."
Yogananda
Contrast that with the Biblical passage:
"Come unto me, all ye that labor and that are heavy laden, and I will give you rest,"
Matthew 11:28.

Here's something I find comforting –
Lean on your faith and your "tribe" (those you trust). Look up the **Serenity Prayer**, read it and apply to your life. Daily.

SERENITY PRAYER

"God grant me the Serenity to accept the things I cannot change, courage to change the things I can and wisdom to know the difference...
Living one day at a time, enjoying one moment at a time, accepting hardships at the pathway to peace, taking, as He did the Sinful world, as it is, not as I would have it: trusting that He will make all things right if I surrender to His will: that I may be reasonably happy in this life and supremely happy with him in the next."
Amen.

Even the US Constitution has a pointed statement in its amendment.

1. Freedom of Religion… "Congress shall make no law respecting an establishment of *religion*… "

The US one dollar bill still declares "In God We Trust," as it has for centuries. Ad infinitum. But do we bother to remember that blatant declaration?

P.S. Remember when there was that popular saying, "In God We Trust… all others pay cash."?

PRAY FOR AMERICA… and the World.

2 Chronicles 7:14 "If then people, upon whom my name has been pronounced, humble themselves and pray, and seek my

face and turn from their evil ways, I will hear them from Heaven and their sins and heal their land."
Spiritual principles endure. They are expressed by new generations in different ways, but the teachings have been around forever. Literally. Pre-millennia and will go on and on...

It's comforting to know these age old expressions of faith and belief will be somewhat contemporary no matter the year or age. Alive and relevant. Rich and powerful. Transferable and precious.

On a seemingly unrelated note, prayer can be actually be diverse in its practice.

OUR WALKS ARE PRAYERS.

A direct way to talk to God- or to listen to Him- is prayer. And meditation. But prayer does not have to be the sitting on your knees by the side of your bed, arms folded and hands clasped together style, which is what perhaps many people see as the only way to pray. "And now I lay me down to sleep..."

At Serra Retreat, and other places of contemplation, labryrinths were created to serve as a place to meditate in motion. The ancient stone-lined tool for spiritual contemplation, the walking pattern in these labyrinths was common across civilizations for more than 4,000 years! – **A "Prayer - in Motion."**

Serra Retreat -   The Labyrinth.
"You Show Me The Path of Life."

The Labyrinth I met at Serra, with its Santa Rosa design, offered a place of quiet. Little did I know with that focused walk around those stones, I was tracing the steps of perhaps hundreds before me in *their* walk with God, and self.

Who knew walking around in circles could be not only be "fun" but spiritually meaningful in an almost "trance"-like way?

As I write this, and as is by some of kind of "God wink," I plan to return to Serra for a Spring retreat this year. (Global Truth Center LA offer this opportunity to all).

In God we trance??

Then there is sitting in prayer and meditating. It is said that prayer is talking to God – or your Higher Power – and meditation is listening to God – or your version of Him. Or Her.

"SIT AT PEACE - PEACE AT YOUR FEET, INFUSE US WITH YOUR PRESENCE – AND EVERYBODY SAID 'AMEN'."

Jesus (Jesus Christ)**'s** name in Hebrew was "Yeshua," which translates in English to "Joshua."

A "Christian" name is that for a person whose given name is that which is distinguished from a family name, last name or "surname." The name Christian means follower of Christ.

The term *"Robbing Peter to Pay Paul"* aka "Maneuvering the Apostles," came from Saints Peter and Saint Paul, meaning taking from one person and giving to another. There are variants in other languages.

The *"Never Look Back"* common phrase has as its origin tracing way back to the Old Testament. The story of Lot's Wife, who tragically and contrary to the orders the guiding angel, whom was supervising Lot's household, indeed looked back and was turned into a salt pillar.

"Christmas" actually means "Mass on Christ's Day," despite being celebrated internationally by Christians and pagans alike.

Ehud is the only person identified as being a "leftie." Judges 3: 12-30, in the Old Testament tells us it is so. His name Biblically means "He who praises."

Haddasah was another name for *Queen Esther* in the Old Testament.

During Ramadan, Muslims over the age of 12 fast from dawn to dusk, and give charity. At the Islamic Center of Conejo Valley, they also recite the Quran in its entirety.

Saint Clare was one the first followers of St. Francis of Assissi and wrote The Rule of Life, the first monastic set of guidelines written by a woman...

FUN FACT! In 1958, Pope Pius XII declared Saint Clare patron of television, citing an incident during her last illness when she miraculously saw the Midnight mass in the basilica of San Francesco on the far side of Assisi at Christmas!

Mother/Sister Teresa (real name Anjeze Gonkxe Bojaxhiu performed miracles for which she was canonized. St. Teresa. The number seven is the most important and featured number in The Bible. It reveals as a wholeness, completeness or completion. Like "On the seventh day God rested," found in Genesis 2 2-3. Numerically, God had a sense of humor.

In the King James version of The Bible, bees were not considered okay to be eaten, but John The Baptist ate them with honey in Matthew 3:4.

There are 3 types of Nuns: Monastic (the most devout), Mendicant (combining monastic and outside life) and Canons and Clerics Regular (who live in the community).

What Four Things Did Mother Teresa, Francis of Assisi, John Paul II, Therese of Lisieux and Ignatius of Loyola have in common? They all practiced the Four Signs: Prayer; Study; Generosity and Evangelization.

Brilliant and prolific painter **Vincent Van Gogh** was a Protestant minister. He was kicked out of the church for not being "eloquent enough."

US President **John F. Kennedy** was the first one to shake hands, rather than kiss the ring of a Pope (John Paul II).

"Lead Me, Guide Me" was the first hymnal commissioned for the African American Catholics. "The song was also something passed down, like faith itself." Vinson Cunningham, The New Yorker, July 15, 2022.

The "House of God" is first and oldest hospital in the world, situated in Paris, next to the Notre Dame Cathedral. "L'Hotel Dieu" was founded in 651 AD by Saint Landry.

Dutch artist **Hieronymous Bosch** was a member of the Brotherhood of Notre-Dame, a devout Christian Catholic. His famous masterpiece, the triptych "The Garden of Earthly Delights" features a figure of God. "Lord, Have Mercy!"

Sinead O'Connor tore up a picture of **Pope John Paul II** (Joannes Paulus II , 1978-2005) live on "Saturday Night Live," as a protest, not so much about the Pope, but about her late mother, and the alleged abuse of the church. She converted to becoming a Muslim...

In France, members of the French National Assembly, or Senate are prohibited from wearing religious attire in state buildings. "America fought a civil war over slavery, France's civil wars were over religion." (The Atlantic, December 2021).

Another Muslim covert (stage name) **Cat Stevens** became **Yusuf Islam**, devoted himself to Allah, but recently reverted to musical roots, re-releasing songs of a more secular nature.

Bette Midler was first cast as nun Sister Mary Clarence in "Sister Act" the movie. Such a hit, it spawned the sequel "Sister Act 2: Back in the Habit."

Christian **Renhold Niebuhr** gave us the Serenity Prayer. The Rev's widely recited prayer was made popular by Alcoholics Anonymous (AA -- not Auto Club – and 12-Step programs.

Oprah Winfrey was named after a biblical figure in the Book of Ruth, "Orpah," her real name. However, her family butchered it, changed it to Oprah and that name caught on. Her birth certificate says "Orpah." (meaning neck or fawn).

"Mr. Rogers" (Fred) was a Christian, with a huge affection for Catholics. He also believed "Peace means far more than the opposite of war."

Charles "Sparky" **Schulz**, "Peanuts" cartoons creator was a devout man of Christ. He loved playing tennis. We met at the delightful Santa Barbara's Writers Conference… Not on the court!... but we did meet Sparky there.

Tom Petty is buried at Lake Shrine, in Los Angeles. There was a private funeral held for the singer there in 2001.

"The Tales of Sherlock Holmes" by **Arthur Conan Doyle** was so popular in the early 1900s, that it replaced The Bible in some hotel rooms in the early 1900s.

The biggest selling author of fiction? Second only to God's Bible? Agatha Christie. Two billion and counting (This was a tweet by my mate Phillip Adams, Australian media personality).

The duo **Air Supply**, (Russell Hitchock and Graham Russell) the Australian soft rock pop sensation of the 1980's, eminated from the cast of the Oz production of "Jesus Christ Superstar."

American Muslims come from diverse backgrounds and are on the most racially diverse religious groups in the US, according to a 2009 Gallup Poll.

20 to 30 percent of enslaved Africans brought to America were Muslim…

Meanwhile, there is a band out of San Diego called The Muslims. "…who clearly don't practice Islam…" (Interview magazine, October 2008).

Psalm 103 1-5 displayed subtly at Sunlife Organics stores, is probably something not everyone would notice. The smoothie and more store popular with the health conscious was founded by Khalil Rafati. He went from living on the streets of Skid Row, LA to recovery and spirituality. The Psalm relates to rebirth. The pink lotus logo/symbol? "From the mud and darkness, grows a beautiful flower."

Mel Gibson's name was derived after St. Mel, the Irish Saint.
Musician **John Tesh** said in Nigeria anyone who is kind and helpful is called "Pastor," and consider dong a ministry. He was surprised by the honor of being called that title , just for being kind… It showed in actions and words.

Pat Benatar has a "Holy 14" songs in her repertoire, including "Invincible." The singer is a lapsed Roman Catholic. Go figure. Music is her go to, rather than religion. Pleasing fans, not God. No judgment…

Pamela Lee ("Baywatch") **Anderson** wanted to be a nun or an archeologist, she said on a CBS "Sunday Morning" program. From one habit to another.

The "Hail Mary" pass in (American) footy popularized in 1975 came from the traditional Catholic prayer in which divine intervention is called from the Virgin Mary.

Pervasive and perhaps subliminal, even my (US) Passport says right there on page 12 "We have a great dream…God grant that America will be true to her dream," **Martin Luther King, Jr.**

St. Paul's Chapel is New York's oldest public building. (Concerts are held on Mondays at 1 pm).

Ever wondered what those fish symbols are on the back of some cars? They're the "Jesus Fish" (or Ichthys, in Greek). Originally adopted by Christians as a silent witness to Jesus since the 1980's.

Certain businesses (retail) like Chik Fil A, and Lassens are closed on Sunday for a reason, not just because they want a "day off." Owner of the former (S. Truett Cathy, a Southern Bapist) saw the importance of closing one day a week to worship, if his employees wished. Lassens? Owner Hilmar Frode Lassen was a Danish Church of Latter Day Saints follower.

The writing in the mezuzah (Jewish doorside) scroll has to be handwritten or it is invalid. "Glory to God Alone" it says.

Westminster Abbey was built as part of a Benedictine Monastery and as a sacred place for the crowing place and burial of English kings and queens. In 1064ish, Monks built a parish church, St. Margaret's, to serve the local Londoners in Westminster. It was dedicated to St. Margaret of Antioch the third St. Margaret's was begun in 1488 and consecreated in 1523.

Pakistan is 98% Muslim. Suprisingly not Hindu. Given its proximity to India. In my humble, uninformed opinion.

The idiom "a leopard never changes its spots"? It can be traced back to the Bible. Jeremiah 13:23. "Can the Ethiopian change his skin, or a leopard, its spots?"

The word "Hare" refers to the divine potency of God.
"Krishna" means the "all attractive one."
("Rama" is the reservoir of all pleasure.")

Hare Krishnas believe that the sound vibration of the mantra has a direct impact on the soul. According to a philosophy of ancient India, the soul is spiritually asleep.

/URBAN YOGA.MELB

Denys Arcand, French-Canadian director of "Jesus of Montreal," raised in a very religious Catholic family, spending 8 years at a Jesuit College.

Contemporary artist **Jean Michel Basquait**, was raised Catholic. "Untitled God/Law" oilstick on paper was one of his most famous and controversial works.

Canadian singer **Justin Bieber** turns to his faith before every concert, with a prayer circle with his band. He said it helped him with his recent illness.

Leon Bloy, underrated French writer and Catholic convert. He underwent a profound religious conversion

Joseph Biden, sitting United States President is a proud Catholic.

Conservative Christian **Pat Boone** known mostly as a singer also acted in "The Cross and the Switchblade" (and "The Eyes of Tammy Faye" doco. in 2000…A feature film based on televangelist Tammy was released the next year starring Jessica Chastain).

Irish American actor **Pierce Brosnan** was brought up by his grandparents who were Roman Catholic.

American basketball legend **Kobe Bryant** was raised Roman Catholic.

Leo "Dr. Love" **Buscaglia**, media guru and author was raised R.C. but influenced by Buddhism. – *"Life is Unchartered Territory. It reveals it's story one moment at a time."*

American actor **Steve Carrell** is a practicing Catholic. He even played the biblical role of Noah in "Evan Almighty."

Jim Carrey, actor and author, was born in Canada and raised Catholic but has explored Scientology, Transcendentalism, Kabala and Christianity. Carrey believes in the motto "Believe in miracles and the belief in the power ofyour own manifestations, and your own faith." Meaning living a life that is moral and "cool."

G. K. Chesterton, Writer and lay Theologian, "orthodox" Christian, converted from Anglican to Catholic.

Former actor, now American TV Show host Stephen Colbert was raised Irish Catholic.

George Clooney, American actor, was raised a strict Catholic but leans towards an Athetist point of view.

American movie star **Leonardo DiCaprio** who is from an Italian background was raised and is a devout Catholic.

The Spokane neighborhood where **Bing Crosby** lived was mainly Catholic and was sometimes referred to as the "Little Vatican," or the "Holy Land." His real name was Harry and the crooner indeed played the role of a priest in "Going My Way," the musical comedy drama film circa 1944.

R.A. Dickey of the NY Mets baseball team went on an extraordinary trek to raise awareness, and funds for Bombay Team Challenge (alleviating women's and children's suffering from abuse and addiction). "God is Good" was the message Dickey sent upon reaching Mt. Kilimanjaro's peak in 2011.

Walt Disney, Congregationalist Christian. Disney was the one who asked of himself to "Live a good Christian Life." And he said "Deeds rather than words express my concept of the part religion should play in everyday life." He also said "Without Divine inspiration, we would all perish."

Fantasia (Barrino) singer. "We were like your church," after her American Idol performance, said Paul Abdul. A "Young Aretha" said Randy Jackson. She is from a gospel singing family.

Jane Fonda a devout Christian "I believe that Christ was the personal incarnation of the divine wisdom in everything, including every form of spiritual expression. I feel like a Christian, I believe in the teachings of Jesus and try to practice them in my life. I found Christians all over this country who feel as I do. They may not be 'saved' yet they hum with divine spirit." She said she really liked this, a quote from Rev. Forrest Church: "God is not God's name, God is our name for that which is greater than them all and yet present in all."

Australian American **Mel Gibson**, actor, is a member of a small sect of Catholicism called Traditional Catholicism.

Hispanic American actress and singer **Selena Gomez** was raised in the Catholic faith. She now attends Hillsong Church in Los Angeles.

English Anthropologist/primatologist (Dame) **Jane Goodall,** reared in a Christian Congregationalist family, studied theosophy. *"I must believe in God.... I don't have any idea of who or what God is, but I do believe in some great spiritual power, particularly when I am out in nature."*

Heidi Hamilton, KLOS radio personality, co host of "The Heidi and Frank Show," was raised a Catholic. She also appeared on the television show "Dish Nation," entertainment news in a comedic format.

American movie star **Tom Hanks**. Raised as a Catholic and Mormon, joined the Greek Orthodox Church upon marrying actress and singer American Greek Rita Wilson. They made "My Big Fat Greek Wedding," the hit movie and the sequel.

American actress **Anne Hathaway** was raised by Catholic parents and even considered becoming a nun. Her family converted to Episcopalianism.

"Everwood" actor and Tony nominated **Anne Heche** once said "God is going to take everyone back to heaven on a spaceship." This from the woman who believed she was a reincarnation of God him/herself. (Her memoir? "Call Me Crazy").

French author **Victor Hugo** identified as a Catholic in his youth but rejected the church and became, in his words, a "freethinker."

Michael Keaton, American actor was raised a Catholic. He starred in the controversial film, "Spotlight," ironically about abuse by Catholic priests.

John F. Kennedy, US President, was a devout Irish Catholic. "There are three things which are real: God, human folly and laughter," Kennedy once said. *"The first two are beyond our comprehension so we much do what we can with the third."*

Edgy **Lady Gaga** (real name Stefani Joanne Angelina Gemanotta), phew! Singer/Actor/Performance Artist. Italian- Catholic reared in New York.

Singer and musician **John Legend** had a Christian upbringing and he claims it inspired may of his songs. Played Jesus in TV's "Jesus Christ Superstar."

American actress **Lindsay Lohan** although raised a Catholic has explored Kabbalah, like Madonna, and Scientology like Nicole Kidman and was rumored to be converting to Islam.

Madonna (Louise Ciccione), Singer/Actor, raised Catholic but dabbled in Kabbalah.

Media personality Bill O'Reilly and author is a devout Catholic.

Willie Nelson was a bible salesman in the 1950's as a young dude. He also wrote a song "Family Bible" in 1957, inspired by his "Rock of Ages" singing grandmother, who also read the Good Book to him.

Dolly Parton, who claims to be "very, very "'Spiritual'" then the big R "Religious." "Find out who you are, and do it on purpose," she once said.

Television journalist **Robin Roberts**, who confessed "I was afraid people couldn't understand I could be Christian and gay."

Mr **(Fred) Rogers** was a devout Christian. He was very unassuming in expressing his faith. But he did. And was loved.

Kenny "I loved going to our church" **Rogers**. (a Baptist believer).

Carlos Santana, Guitar "God" believes in the *"man Upstairs"* and finds solace in Him. His music is very spiritual.

Martin Scorsese is a devout Catholic. His film, "The Last Temptation of Christ," rocked the religious boat.

Late Dodgers announcer **Vin Scully**, was a devout Catholic, and he went to Mass on his way to the ballgame apparently (at nearby his home, the St. Judes church, in Westlake Village).

Arnold Schwarzenegger, the former Austrian bodybuilder, movie star and former California Governor was rumored to have been raised Catholic.

Maria Shriver, ex-spouse of *Arnold Schwarzenegger*'s married him at St. Francis Catholic church, Hyannis, Massachusetts.

Jessica Simpson, American media personality, reared a Baptist.

"Catholic kid" **Sting** (real name *Gordon Sumner*) is apparently agnostic according to a Time magazine interview, the "certainties of a religion are 'dangerous'." His songs like "All This Time" tell a different story.

William Ashley "Billy" Sunday was an American baseball player who became a celebrated Christian evangelist.

Ivana Trump was "secretly raised" Catholic. Husband, Donald, claims he is a "Prezzie" (Presbyterian). They were married by Protestant clergyman Norman Vincent ("The Power of Positive Thinking") Peale.

Actor **Mark Wahlberg** ("Father Stu') Catholic was raised in Boston and is a devout man of God.

American (Pop) artist **Andy Warhol**, was raised in the Byzantine Catholic faith by his Czech family.

Oprah Winfrey is proud that she reads the bible and prays on her knees daily.

Alfre Woodard, played Winnie Mandela, she attended Catholic school in Oklahoma.

Wynonna, (singer) as in Judd, thanks the Lord for His grace and His mercy. "My heart, my soul, my faith, my hopes and dreams, my family, my home, my friends, my enemies, my music, my life- I thank you for helping me face the truth."

("Revelations" CD liner notes, ©Curb Music Company/MCA Records Inc.)

Catherine Zeta Jones Welsh actress raised Catholic when she married actor Michael Douglas who is Jewish. They raised their children using messages from both faiths.

Naomi Judd singer "Having explored all the world's major religions, I've chosen Jesus Christ to be my personal mentor, teacher, and savior. I have an unshakable faith as a Christian."

A little PS (or "PTL"!)... **Jessica Chastain**, raised with Christ who played infamous televangelist **Tammy Faye**, "She just loved everyone, and she loved without judgment and she believed everyone was deserving of God's grace," Chastain said in an interview. "Now I wasn't baptized. But I think that's supposed to be what Christianity is about."

Alanis Morrisette, Canadian/American singer, songwriter and actor. Raised Catholic. Became a Buddhist. And a minister.

David Bowie, English singer, actor and artist. Bowie also experimented with multiple other religions and faiths.
Jeff Bridges, American actor and photographer.
John Cleese, British actor (reputedly).
America's **Richard Gere**, actor (widely known as a Buddhist).
Goldie Hawn, US actor and Producer (raised Jewish Presbyterian who was later drawn to Buddhism).
Apple's **Steve Jobs.** His Buddhist principles influenced his Apple products apparently.

Self described "Buddhist Methodist" **George Lucas**, "Star Wars" movie Producer.

Orlando Bloom has practiced Buddhism since he was a teenager.

Tina Turner, resilient and powerful late American singer (devotedly for many years). The Queen of Rock!

Amy Jordan, American dancer, choreographer and motivational speaker (inspirational)!!

Alanis Morrisette, Canadian singer and songwriter. Also an ordained minister of Universal Life Church.

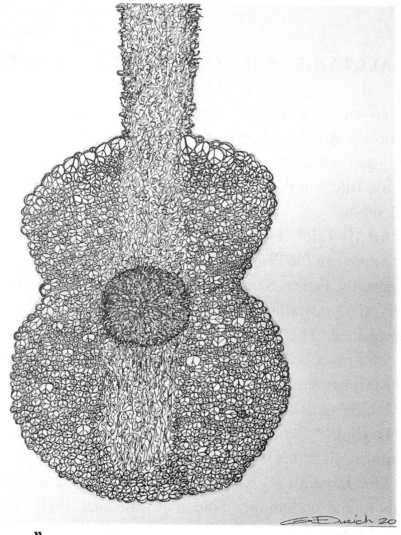

"Instrument of Peace" (Pen & Ink) by the Author

"The greatest aid to...keeping God in memory is perhaps music." Swami Vivekananda
I was tempted to call this the "Pulpit Playlist," but it is so much more than Church music. (Albeit the attractive alliteration!). Here are songs with stories.

ALL LYRICS ARE COPYRIGHT BY THE ARTIST.

Aerosmith's **"Adam's Apple"** is the band's version of Bible's Adam and Eve story in Genesis 3. Steven Tyler (singer and songwriter wanted to dub the album "Love at First Bite," in this vein after the line "Lordy it was love at first bite."

"All My Life" K-Ci & Jojo Gorgeous God praise!

"American Pie" Don McLean. "And the three men I admire most, the Father, Son and the Holy Ghost..." This and other cryptic lyrics alluded to God. In a interview, McLean also explained "The Jester stole his thorny crown..." was to do with Jesus Christ on the Cross - and Bob Dylan.

"Blasphemous Rumors" A very dark but powerful Depeche Mode song. Almost "cinematic" in its storyline.

"Daylight" David Kushner. This song and his others are influenced by his strong faith in God.

"The Dreaming" Kate Bush. Based on the concept of aboriginal mythology. Title song from her 1980's album. Highly spirited!

Norman Greenbaum's **"Spirit in the Sky"** – "Gotta have a friend in Jesus….I got a friend in Jesus."

"Fire and Rain"("You've Got to look down upon me Jesus…") James Taylor. American-Australian Marcia Hines does a praiseworthy sensational cover version.

"Free Fallin'" Tom Petty. Raised Southern Baptist, not a practicing Christian. Bob Dylan described him as being "full of the light." Of Jesus? "She's a good girl, loves her mama, loves Jesus and America too.."

"From A Distance" Bette Midler ("God is Watching Us" with Radio Choir of New Hope Baptist Church).

"God," John Lennon/Plastic Ono Band. (Irreverent, and blasphemous, unlike "Give Peace A Chance," which was anti "ism's" and Hare Krisna-conscious).

"God & Love," Boy George and Culture Club. Hypnotic song and simple truthful, powerful message.

"God Bless the Child" James Taylor and Billie Holiday. Shows off beautiful simplicity.

"God Only Knows" The Beach Boys song also wonderfully covered by none other than David Bowie. Melodically beautiful, and unexpected in secular music. – Christian band For King and Country have a more confronting version of their own. Listen to it!

"God Willing…" Johnny Cash. Classic country song about religion and God.

"God's Country" Blake Sheldon, countryish twang storytelling of Baptism and more…

"Good For Me," Amy Grant, crossover Christian/secular singer. A slew of hits, pop-py but heartfelt. "Queen of Christian Pop."

"If I Die When I'm High, (I'll Be Halfway to Heaven)" Micah and Willie Nelson collaboration. God bless son who wrote this ditty and his father who sings along. "The gospel is Willie's lens," says Country Thang Daily.

"Hallelujah" Leonard Cohen (Well maybe there's a God above....). Cohen song covered over and over....

"Have A Little Faith In Me" John Hiatt (covered by Cocker, as in Joe). Belief and faith after addiction. Matthew 8:26 - "Ye of little faith..."

"Higher Ground," written and performed by Stevie Wonder "Believers, keep on believing." Red Hot Chili cover this song with brilliantly!

"Holy Mother" Eric Clapton (about Mother Church- Virgin Mary), with help from Luciano Pavarotti and East London Gospel Choir sung at a Benefit in Bosnia. (Pavarotti had his own song).

"House of the Lord" Phil Wickham. Rousing song about worshipping God, praise and forgiveness.

"If Ever I Lose My Faith" Sting. A lot to say about faith, and losing it. In relationships and "self."

"I Believe in Jesus" Donna Summer. Interpreted by Summer. "Ran into Mother Mary down on Vine Street in L.A." (In the musical of her life and music and "The Wanderer" album of 1980.

"I Guess The *Lord* Must Be In New York City," Harry Nillson. Another reason to love the Big Apple.

"I'll Be Missing You" Puff Daddy. Moving and prayerful twist to The Police's song "Every Breath.."

"In The Air Tonight" Despite the ambiguous interpretations and his spiritual "middle-of-the roadness" regarding faith, English singing drummer Phil Collins sure shows up with some spiritual lyrics in some of his songs. …"Oh Lord, I've been waiting for this moment all my life." It appears the hit tune is about a marital rift. On the same "Face Value" release, he sings "Oh God I hope it's not late (in "The Roof is Leaking"). His band Genesis asks "Do You Believe in God?" in the urgent song "Jesus He Knows Me." It is about televangelism spreading false hope.

"Presence of the Lord" by Blind Faith, Eric Clapton and cohorts. A searing song that screams Christian faith. *Cream* of the crop.

"Into My Arms" Nick Cave & the Bad Seeds' "I don't believe in an interventionist God…" (recommended by writer and actor mate Daniel Lillford from Oz, now of Nova Scotia, Canada).

"Jesus, Are You There?," The Babys. An acerbic faith and belief in Jesus and other faiths, including Hare Krishnas.

"Jesus is Just Alright" Doobie Bros. (Loving Jesus? A mainstream hit, but remake of a gospel song by Art Reynolds). Also done by The Byrds… Even better still!

"Jesus is the Light 0f the World" Aretha Franklin (recorded in L.A., heard first at Atmosphere, loved by

Randy…and me. Gospel rocks!...Pastor Kevin Nickerson, Rams chaplain, "old school black church" shared "Jesus is the Light of the World" was played after services).

"Jesus Take The Wheel" Carrie Underwood. Storytelling with a twang, and deep at that. Let go, and let God seems to be the message.

"King of My Heart" Sarah and John McMillan. Rousing Christian song of hope and faith.

"Levon" Elton John's odd but beautiful song is open to interpretation. References to Jesus and God ("is dead") are freeform. Who knows what it means.

"Like A Prayer" Madonna (pop-ish song, but building up to a full blown gospel choir back up). Almost as controversial as her **"Papa Don't Preach"** (delving into her Catholic roots).

"Like Jesus to a Child" George Michael (was he leaning into "Faith"? We'll never know).

"Livin' on a Prayer" Bon Jovi (secular or spiritual?). Dynamite song regardless!

"Mercedes Benz" "Oh Lord won't you buy me a Mercedes Benz? I'm counting on you Lord, please don't let me down…" Janis Joplin. Cover versions have included Elton John and Pink. And its been featured in ads. (Co written by Bob Neuwirth).

"Love God, Love People" Danny Gokey. American Idol contestant incredible Christian song. Wow, just wow.

"Mona Lisa and Mad Hatters" Another Elton John one. "Thank the Lord…" By Bernie Taupin. about NYC.

"Mrs. Robinson," Folk rock duo Paul Simon and Art Garfunkel's tune from the '60s. Lyrics, "God Bless You Please, Mrs. Robinson, heaven holds a place for those who pray, Jesus loves you more than you will know."

"My Lord What a Mornin'," Harry Belafonte. Ageless spiritual and a song of hope.

"My Main Man/There Is A God," Staple Singers. Gospel song about the good Lord. Great vocal and tune.

"My Sweet Lord (Hare Krisna)," George Harrison, Hare Krisna. (Chant "I really want to see you, My Sweet Lord) A Mega Hit....

"Oh My Lord," Ringo Starr (Well intentioned song with unlikely theme from this not too "deep" Beatle).

"Only God Can Judge Me," Tupac Shakur. Song that ebbs and flows like the tides of the ocean. "Parental Advisory! Explicit lyrics!!

"Only The Good Die Young," 'You Catholic Girls Start Much Too Late" croons Billy Joel, in this hit, which continues with the rosary and "crying with Saints."

"Salvation" The Cranberries. This song speaks not only to the negative repercussions of drug use but it could also be about the free gift of salvation Jesus Christ gives us.

"Say A Little Prayer" Aretha Franklin (she was a church singer initially, afterall)... secular or Spiritual?

"Save A Prayer" Duran Duran (unlikely song from a pop band who were areligious, about a one night stand).

"Say It Loud…" Godfather of Soul James Brown "Ooh wee Oh Lord…you're killing me."

"Serve Somebody," Bob Dylan (his foray in Christianity. "It may be Devil, it may be the Lord.."

"God Only Knows," sings James Taylor in his beautiful ballad **"Song For You Far Away."**

"That's Why God Made The Movies," by the singer with probably the most Biblical name ever, Paul Simon.

"Wear You Love Like Heaven" Donovan "Lord Kiss Me Once More Fill Me With Song, Allah, Kiss Me Once More, That I May…" "Be Heavenly and Turn Off Your Mind for a Pause…"

"What if God Was One of Us?" Joan Osborn (a tongue in cheek take on the Lord) "like a stranger on a bus…"

"The Wind" Cat Stevens/Yusuf ("Where I'll end up, well I Think Only God Really Knows….)… also **"Morning Has Broken"** covered by Cat. "God's recreation of the new day" is such a beautiful lyric. A hymn.

"Personal Jesus" Depeche Mode (covered by Johnny Cash astonishingly enough). Based on "Elvis and Me," by Priscilla P. "Someone to hear your prayers, someone who cares."

"Please, Please Let Me Get What I Want," Morrissey. Oh Lord… a melodic song from the Catholic Smiths singer.

"Praise The Lord" Breland featuring Thomas Rhett, semi sacreligious country song about random things from the South. Message of gratitude though!

"River" Leon Bridges. Christian faith was his salvation, as he rose from dishwasher to successful soul singer.

"Unanswered Prayers" Garth Brooks. A Christian country song about remorse.

"More Than Anything" Anita Wilson. Heard at Atmosphere service. Rocking gospel.

"Living Hope" Another Atmosphere favorite, by Bethany Wohrle. Almost sounding like "Baptist gospel" in its Hallelujah's!

"5 Foot 9" "God made the good stuff," in this Tyler Hubbard country tune.

"Thankful" Verses, an Australian band now in Nashville.

"W.M.A" Intense driving tune by Pearl Jam. "Jesus greets me, looks just like me…"

"God Makes Me Want To Sing" by Daniel Nahmod, heard at Global Truth Center. Very uplifting and rather different from Stryper (the Christian metal band from the "O.C")'s "(Jesus) Makes Me Wanna Sing." Both valid. He played beautifully at Unity of the Oaks, Thousand Oaks also.

"Kumbaya, My Lord" Creole Gullah hymn, call to God to come and help the people as they faced oppression. Lightness with power!

"Viva La Vida" Coldplay. I could've sworn the lyrics were "Roman *Catholic* Choirs are singin'" Instead, it's "Roman Calvary Choirs are…" Chris Martin's song is about the dethroning of Jesus. "I know St. Peter Won't Call My Name."

"Does anyone know where the love of God goes when the waves turn the minutes to hours?" great lyric from "The Wreck of the Edmund Fitzgerald,"
Gordon Lightfoot.

... Sometimes music just makes sense of everything. As Pastor Tom Eyre, Atmosphere fill-in Pastor, formerly of City Church, Ventura, said "I'm thankful for this music. It makes me feel spiritual!"

"May God's Love (Lift Off) Be With You…"
David Bowie, "Space Oddity," 1969

"Faith films are Here to Stay,"
"Jesus Revolution" promotional slogan.

"A Beautiful Day in the Neighborhood," Tom Hanks embodies "Mister Rogers."At the core of the movie is forgiveness and kindness. No special effects or car chases. Simple.

"Ben Hur," the 1959 Biblical epic starring Charleton Heston made Academy awards history by winning 11 awards for one picture.

"Boy Erased," controversial film with Nicole Kidman about a church-supported gay conversion program. Spoiler Alert: Baptist preacher unwillingly participates.

"God's Not Dead," Subtitled "A Light In Darkness," powerful lesson about family and church for our times.

"Honk for Jesus. Save Your Soul," a comedy about the pastor of a megachurch, who after a sex scandal, attempts to rebuild the congregation with the help of his wife. Sidenote: We went to see the "Top Gun sequel "Maverick," and were told it was sold out. And we were instead issued free tickets to "Honk for Jesus..." We ended up seeing the "Top Gun" movie with the "...Jesus" tickets! Another Godwink??

"Jesus Revolution," Set in the 1970's street preacher opens doors of his crumbling church to a sea of young folk. "The greatest spiritual awakening in America of the century."
"Mission:Joy," Netflix doco. Dalai Lama meets Bishop Tutu. Buddhist and Christian, brothers in faith and love.
"Witness," Peter Weir directed classic, depicting Amish folk. Weaving in drama, suspense and romance. Actor Harrison Ford as an unwitting "yonie" (Yehonatan) is unforgettable…and hilarious.
"John Tesh: Worship at Red Rocks," Music and more, including production pics for your screensaver! (gardencitymusic.com)

"This is not just Christian 'entertainment' – but built on rock, not sand that can be washed away." Atmosphere Church bandleader

.

CATHOLIC CINEMA-
A SELECT LIST

"Agnes of God," starring Anne Bancroft and Jane Fonda based on the play. A powerful story about nuns and virginal conception.

"Doubt," A Father (Philip Seymour Hoffmann) and Meryl Streep as Mother Superior battle it out over treatment of boys in a Catholic school in America circa 1964.

"The Devil's Playground," Powerful Australian drama directed by Fred Schepisi about boy's coming of age in Catholic boarding school (semi autobiographical).

"Father Stu," Based on a true story, a faith based film, still cheerful, irreverent and unpreachy," according to one of its stars. Jackie Weaver. Mark Wahlberg plays the lead.

"Novitiate," A young woman believes she's been called by Jesus to become a Nun, during second Vatican Council in the '60's.

"Nuns on the Run," British comedy starring Eric Idle about a couple of London gangsters who plan to rob a gang of their ill gotten money.

"Sister Act" (and **"Sister Act 2,"** Fun with the nuns, black and white. Starring Whoopi Goldberg as Deloris, and Maggie Smith as Mother Superior.

"Spotlight," Drama about Catholic priests' abuse investigated by Boston newspaper. Michael Keaton and Mark Ruffalo star.

"The Thornbirds," Catholic priest meets woman, romance and drama ensues. Another Australian work, based on the brilliant best seller by author Colleen McCullough.

"The Chosen," first-ever multi-season US TV show about the life of Jesus. Said to be created outside the Hollywood system, the series allows us to see Him through the eyes of those who knew Him.

"Brides of Christ," Australian/Irish miniseries about Catholic nuns and their minors (girls), set in 1960's rural Australia. Bittersweet tales of coming of age.

"Teresa of Avila," Drama about Spain's nun and mystic St. Teresa of Jesus. Intense but well worth watching.

"With This Light," moving documentary about Sister Maria Rosa Leggol, who dedicated her life to Honduran orphans and abandoned children.

FAMOUS INSPIRATIONS

Saint Teresa; Mahatma Gandhi; *Bono*...

"This one thing I do, forgetting those things which are behind, and reaching forth unto those things which are before." Phillipians 3:13

PERSONAL SPIRITUAL INSPIRATIONS

Colleen Coghlan: Family/friend- good Catholic gal. An inspiration and long-time positive influence.
Sai Chadavankar, Meditation guru and friend.
Pastor Jim Crews; and Pastor" Phil" Robilert (a former Catholic and wonderful Senior Pastor), Atmosphere Church. Ying and Yang. Humorous and vibrant.

Pastor Tim Delkeskamp, Ascension Lutheran Senior Pastor. Aka "P.T." You are unforgettable. Such a support and wonderful listener.

Dr. Rev. Gary Dickey, Retired, United Methodist Church. Always chipper!

Don Franz, Presbyterian-raised New York entertainment producer (who provided a *great* story about "Eid Mubarak"). That's the spirit!

Randy Kappen, Friend; Man of God. Providing me with spiritual sustenance especially on Monday evenings.

Reverend Milun Kostic, St. Sava Serbian Orthodox Church, London. ("Hvala") I'll never forget Ladbroke Grove, North Kensington. And my London home and family.

Dr. James Mellon, Global Truth Center, Los Angeles. Direct, deep and funny. I took a shine to him from the get-go. *

Pastor Willis Moerer, Our wedding Minister. Kind and "there" literally…at the proverbial eleventh hour.

Rev. Dr. Sue Rubin: Science of Mind Minister, whose words profoundly influenced me. She spoke to me without knowing it. And helped me realize I was not invisible.

Father Charlie Smiech and Sister Carol Quinlivan, Serra Retreat, Malibu. Warm and caring souls.

Father Jim Strehy, St Jude's. Keep up the humor! I miss you some Sundays.

Seth Wegher Thompson, who encouraged me to explore Catholicism in a deeper way and invited me in. A trusted friend. Thank you.

"We find after years of struggle, that we do not take a trip; a trip takes us." John Steinbeck

*Global Truth Center Los Angeles' motto : We affirm:

"RIGHT WHERE I AM, GOD IS.'

OUR VISION IS *TO: "LOVE ONLY, FORGIVE EVERYTHING, AND REMEMBER WHO YOU ARE."*

SPECIAL THANKS

Kitty Dill-Durich: I am particularly grateful to my loving spouse and brilliant editor. And "publicist." With time, love and attention to detail, help make it happen.
Craig Leener: A huge shout out. For your belief in me. And to keep going with this "crazy" book idea.
Lissa Coffey: A woman I've long admired. Creative, spiritual and talented. Deepak Chopra devotee, to boot.
Jim Lockard: Lyon-based wise teacher and inspiration. Whenever you come to California, and speak, you make me think.
Rob Rodriguez: Brother in Christ, friend. A "paramount" influence. *"It is Written... Everything You Speak." Isaiah 40 : 28-31*
John Conley: Author; Artist; Friend and Confidant. Thanks for offering to format and to proof.
Danny Chulak: A gutsy guy who isn't afraid to express himself. And doesn't care about being judged.
Phillip Adams: Broadcaster, author, mentor and "media mate". You taught me more than you'll ever know.

"In Jesus Christ we have the power to become children of God! We can love as he loves, be holy as he is holy, we can share in his divine nature! If we take his hand and follow

him, we can walk by his light, and he will lead us to eternity, to the love that never ends."
"En Jesucristo, tenemos el poder." Archbishop Jose H. Gomez, Mass for the Jubilee Year, 2021.

Multimedia

Affirm Films (Christian film studio)
Relevant Radio (Catholic radio station)
Air 1 (Christian based music and more)
Lighthouse Catholic Media
The Catholic Café, EWTN Radio on Sirius XM (130)
Unity On Line Radio
Word on Fire Catholic Ministries
KFI AM (Coast to Coast, George Noori hosts)

Podcasts

Finding My Religion- Ben Goldstein's romp through all things spiritual. High on the enjoyable list.
5 Minutes in Church History- if you've ever attended church, you may wonder why things happen the way they do. This is blog's for you. Hosted by Stephen Nichols.
Air 1 Pastor's Roundtable- thought provoking talk.
"Bible in a Year," Father Mike Schmitz. Essential for understanding the "good book."
"The Daily Meditation Podcast." Salvation Army. Sip...om

David C. Smalley. Skeptic comedian wants to know why you believe your beliefs.

"Not So Molly Mormon," about all things ex-Mormon. Joseph Smith, founder of Church of Jesus Christ of Latter-Day Saints, would be turning over in his grave! A fresh start in faith, a core disillusioned.

"How Can I Help?" Podcast series by Catholic educated Caitlin McHugh Stamos (wife of John Stamos). Very sincere and enlightening. (Citizens of Sound). Apple Podcasts.

Reverend Graeme blogspot. Inspirational and eclectic wisdom. Revgraeme.blogspot.com

ONLINE   Internet Sites

www.afaithfulversion.org (Christian Biblical Church)

www.agodman.com

www.agodman.com

www.alivethemovement.com

www.ananda.org

www.ANF.org (America Needs Fatima)

www.angelus.com

www.arcchurches.com (Association of Related Churches, to which Atmosphere Church belongs)

www.autom.com (religious apparel, items including holy water bottles and mini saints magnets, stickers and more).

www.catholicallyear.com Get your very own mug of the month! With inspirational saint and Bible verses - and beautiful art.

www.christianity.com

www.churchathome.org

www.companionsofstanthony.org

www.ConvergeMidAmerica.org 21 Day Transformational prayer information. See Bibliography for more.

www.emahofoundation.org (Zachoeje Rinpoche series about Buddhism. Great teaching series).

www.fatherpeyton.org (The "Rosary Priest).

www.flameoflove.us

www.flocknote.com Find a Church on this database which helps it and others reach out to congregations.

www.formed.org (Catholic content free for parishioners – need a parish zip code and name and email to enjoy audio and video programs).

www.FranciscanMedia.org

www.gardencityproject.org (More than 25 Courses on Music, Bible and Worship. And even more!).

www.globaltruthcenter.org

www.hramvaskrsenja.me

www.hsrcenter.com (Holy Spirit Retreat Center, Los Angeles)

www.innerTraditions.com (Books etc.)

www.joniandfriends.org (see below)

www.jw.org (Jehovah's Witnesses)

www.lifewithoutlimbs.org

www.onelifeLA.org

www.sermon central.com

www.serraretreat.com

www.truthofgod.org

www.truthtidbits.com

www.pastors.com

www.pastorrick.com

www.richarddawkins.net

info@meditateinwestlake.org

www.moamerica.org (The Muslims of America, Inc.)

www.limitlesspracticalmuslim.com "Before I 'I Do'"150 Q's Muslims *must* ask pre-marriage

www.skyusa.org (meditation, yoga and spirituality outfit).

www.theoriginalbiblerestored.org

www.unitymagazine.org ; www.unity.org/prayer - also www.unityonlineradio.org
www.usccb.org (United States Conference of Catholic Bishops)
www.sndusa.org (Sisters of Notre Dame)
www.spirituallifemedia.com

TheChristianBeat.org (new music, interviews and events)
www.FathersLoveLetter.com (Page 44)
www.WhyCatholic.com
And last but by no means least,
www.neweraspirituality.com - their mission is simple- To save the world! (Rabbi Ben Goldstein of "Finding My Religion" podcast).

"Philosophy in India is what it ought to be, not the denial, but the fulfillment of religion; it is the highest religion; and the oldest name of the oldest system of philosophy in India is Vedanta, that it, the end, the goal, the highest object of the Vedas"

Friedrich Max Muller

"Stopped into a church, I passed along the way..."
"California Dreamin'"
(The Mamas and The Papas)

"Attend a church, synagogue, or spiritual service, at your destination" suggests Thor Challgren in "Best Vacation Ever." "This may not be everyone's preference on vacation, but again it can be interesting to see how religious services are observed away from home." It reminded me of when I went to a Baptist church in Washington DC, solo, and was the only white worshipper there. The folks not only welcomed me with open arms - they even gave me a

Christmas card. And the gospel music? Spectacular!! Why not spend some time with like minded, righteous believers somewhere meaningful, and safe? And all this for a tithe... and some time.

I visited almost every church in Vienna, Austria. Thor was right. It was meaningful and amazing to experience. And belong to, albeit briefly. Amen.

- Order of Christian Initiation of Adults (OCIA). At the time of writing, this changed from RCIA (Rite of Christian Initiation of Adults) to OCIA. (For budding Catholics wanting to convert).

- Los Angeles Restoration Church. Dedicated to serve the people of the City of Los Angeles. Church phone is (323) 235-4615 or (323) 231-7219, Christian Live-in Home for Men.

- In Touch Ministries leads people worldwide into a growing relationship with Jesus and to strengthen the local church.

- Family Theater Productions. Faith based film company, Creates films, television and digital media programs. Collaborate or just join in their mission by donating.

- Franciscan Monastery of the Holy Land in America. Serve the Holy Land and its people, by becoming a Holy Land Franciscan Friar. Lay down your life for the sake of the Christians who struggle to remain in the Holy Land, serve the pilgrims who are there to deepen their faith and to preserve holy sites that are most important to the Christian faith. Learn more at MyFranciscan.org/vocations.

- Bluejay House Ministries, carrying a heart for ministering to Jesus and cultivating his presence through worship. Lubbock, Texas www.thebluejayhouse.com
- Life Without Limbs. You can make a difference by reviving hope in desperate souls. Donate today! www.lifewithoutlimbs.org (Nick Vujicic's mission).
- I-Godit.com – maybe somewhat random here, but fun bracelets to show your love for the Almighty. (who knew 7-11 was a "spiritual"l store?! Not this guy). A percentage of the proceeds go to the National Suicide Prevention Lifeline, Drug Free America Foundation Inc and the ASPCA for the Prevention of Cruelty to Animals. Steve Mason, founder: "Your confidence comes through faith." (There are also T shirts on the organization's website to order. Subliminal, in their message,maybe, but assured nonetheless)… "No God, No Worries, Know God, No Worries." (Klever Media Corp.)
- Unity (church) offers loving, caring, confidential prayer support. Call (816) 969 2000, or write to Unity Prayer Ministry, 1901 NW Blue Parkway, Unity Village, MO 64065-0001
- The University Series (www.theuniversityseries.org): workshop series

MORE IDEAS –

Participate in **World Day of Prayer**. *Unite with Unity World Day of Prayer. In 2023 this was on March 3... visit www.go.unity.org/wdop for the next one!*

Host a "rosary rally" in your hometown! (Spread the message of Our Lady of Fatima) . Call 1(888)317- 5571 (yours truly did!). When I got a return call, I was called "*'Brother* Gordon," which was sweet. And most certainly unexpected!

If you're newly Christian and need help to grow your faith in God, consider contacting Joni and Friends, founded by Joni Eareckson. The inspirational woman behind this organization and International Disability Center is a tonic. The organization will inspire you to find a church where God can use you in His Kingdom...www.joniandfriends.org (write to Joni and Friends, P.O. Box 3333, Agoura Hills, CA 91376 USA).

The Black Sheep Harley Davidson for Christ Motorcycle Ministry is family-oriented. This organization rides as single adults and married couples (often with children). Some of their events include Blessing of the Bikes, Bible Study at The Bikes, Pop-Up events feeding the homeless and visits to hospitals to pray for downed bikers. They welcome other Harley Davidson (HOG) motorcyclists. Black SheepHDFC.org is a 501©3 non-profit operation supported by its memberships, friends of Black Sheep and local churches. www.BlacksheepHDFC.org

Consider a retreat at many centers, for example Franciscan Renewal Center, Scottsdale, Arizona. Great atmosphere and rates for overnight stays. You do not have to be Catholic! Or Mission San Luis Rey retreat, Oceanside, California. Gorgeous setting and healing of the soul - and mind. Not everyone's spiritual cup of tea.

Last but not least, support and use businesses (local) who are faith based. They can be found at the back of the weekly church bulletin - or business owners displaying the "fish" symbol on their vehicles or on their office or store windows.

"Heaven Means to be One With God." Confucious

Abba – in the Bible means "Father." (Not the name of the 1980's Swedish super pop group!)

Aborigines - People who have been in a country or region since the earliest times. Australian etc.

Absolution - formal release from guilt, obligation, or punishment.

Agape – the love of God for man/kind.

Agnostic-person who neither believes nor disbelieves in a God or religious doctrine.

Amen- concluding word as a response to prayer (Christian, Jewish and Islamic).

Amish- traditional Anabaptist Christian followships with Swiss German (and Alsation) origins. Live interdependently.

Ananda- global movement based on teachings of Paramahansa Yogananda.

Anti-semitism – A hatred of jews.

Ashram- House of God (in Sanskrit).

Atheist-person who does not believe in God/s.

Baptize/baptism- religious rite involving water, symbolizing purification, regeneration and admission into the Christian church.

Bar/Bat Mitzvah- The religious ceremony in which a 13 year old boy/12 year old girl is regarded ready to observe religious precepts, and is eligible to take part in public worship.

Bible- the book of God/ King James Version.

Bhagavad Gita- Hindu religious text or scripture.

Buddha – Ascetic and spiritual teacher of ancient India.

Candidate- A baptized person from another mainline Christian faith. (The baptisms are regarded as valid, so there is no need to re-baptize).

Cardinal-Senior member of the Clergy of the Catholic Church. Created by the Pope.

Catechumen – A non-baptised person who has been through the Rite of Acceptance in the Catholic Church.

Catechism- a summary of Christian principles, in Q's and A's, used for the instruction of both Catholic and Orthodox.

Catholic (kinds) – cradle/convert= born or changed to Catholicism afterwards

Christian- one who believes in Jesus Christ and follows His teachings.

Christo Vero Regi- "For Christ, the True King."

Cloister-covered walkway in Convent, Monastery, or Cathedral.

Conclave-gathering of the (Sacred) "college" of Cardinals. Body of all Catholic Church Cardinals.

Confession- to acknowledge sin to God or to a priest to receive the confession of a penitent).

Confirmation - the rite at which baptized person is admitted as a full member of the church (Christian).

Contrition – Act of - Christian prayer genre that expresses sorrow for sins. Liturgical service or performed in private (special ones used in Catholic, Angelican, Methodist and Reformed Churches (in Catholic, is part of the Sacrament of Penance).

A Course in Miracles - a direct communication from God through Jesus Christ. International course in training your mind to undo the way you see the world.

Covenant-Agreement or maybe a law.

Deism-Existence of God solely based on rational thought, without any reliance on religion or revealed religious authority.

Devout-Having deep religious commitment.

Divinity –The state or quality of being divine.

Eid Mubarak-Muslim Holiday Festival, Festival of the Sacrifice, colloquially "Big Eid."

Elect- A Catechumen who has celebrated the Rite of Election and will receive the Sacraments of Initiation at Easter.

Erasmus – Scholar and clergyman who was the chief leader of Christian humanism, translated the Bible into the vernacular.

Eschatology-Part of theology concerned with destiny.

Freethinker/Freethought-Epistemological viewpoint holds beliefs shoukd be reached by logic, reason and empirical observation. Today, is linked with deism, secularism, atheism, agnosticism and anti-clericalism. And religious critique.

Genuflect- lower one's body in worship.

Godparent- A Catholic who has celebrated all the Sacraments of Initiation an is living the faith, who stands witness for the Sacraments of Baptism and Confirmation.

Gospel- the teaching or revelation of Christ.

Heaven- the abode of God, the angels, and the spirits of the righteous after death; the place or state of existence of the blessed after the mortal life. (The "ultimate party," per Cindy, OCIA, St. Jude of the Apostle).

Hell- The afterlife in which evil souls are subjected to punitive suffering..

Heresy – Belief that differs from the accepted teachings of a religion.

Holy- used in Old Testament to describe God and distinct from us. In the New Testament, applied to people who follow Jesus and want Him to be at work in their lives.

Homily- Religious discourse, rather than a sermon. Intended primarily for spiritual edification.

Indulgence – A pardon from the Catholic Church for a person's sins. The church sold the pardons

Inquisition – The church court that tried people suspected of heresy.

Inquirer- A non baptized person in the beginnings of searching the Catholic faith

Jesus Christ – First century religious leader revered in Christianity, one of the world's major religions and is regarded by most Christians as the incarnation of God.

Kadam- Those who teach the Buddhist scriptures (bka-transmitted word) through personal instructions (gdams-teach/ing).

Karma- action; "what goes around…"

Kirtan- Hindu devotional singing and instrument playing.

Koran- the Muslim bible.

Krishna – Major deity in Hinduism. He is worshipped as the eighth avatar of Vishnu and also as the supreme God in his own right.

Kundun- "Presence," title by which the Dalai Lama is addressed.

Labyrinth- Meditative prayer circle. Santa Rosa design, like at Serra Retreat (stones)- most recognized. Chartres design

(French) like at St. Maxillian Kobe church (one of the most walked).

Manna (also Mana)- Means "what is it? (in Arabic and in Greek and Hebrew). Also, food God provided for the Israelites.

Maranatha- "Our Lord, Come!" Aramaic

Martin Luther – Monk who challenged the Roman Catholic Church and started the Reformation.

Mass- Central act of worship in Catholic church (from "ite, missa, est."Latin- "Go, it is the sending (dismissal).

Maya- Sanskrit for "illusion." "We are nothing but ocean. At the same time, we are also waves."

Menonite- Similar beliefs to Amish. Difference being can use electricity, telephones and motorized vehicles.

Metaphysical- Beyond physical or material.

Mezuzah- 'Doorpost' (Hebrew) encased scroll to remind Jews of their obligation to God.

Monotheism – Belief in a singular God.

Monsignor- Various senior Roman Catholic positions, such as a prelate or an officer of the papal court.

Mosque- Place of prayer for Muslims.

Mullah-Muslim religious teacher.

Muslim- Those adhering to Islam, an Abrahamic religion. They consider the Quran, the central religious text of Islam, to be the verbatim word of the God of Abraham.

Namaste- in Hindu, "Greetings to you."

Neophyte- A newly baptized or received member of the Catholic Church.

Novena- 9 day prayer period leading up to between Good Friday and "Divine Mercy" Sunday.

Omnism- recognition of all religion/s

Orthodox offshoot of Catholic. Russian, Greek – of Alexandria; Antioch; Jerusalem, Serbian, Coptic, Armenian, and Bulgarian: Ukrainian, Polish, Estonian, Latvian, Finland (Finnish?) ….

Paganism – Term first used by early Christians for people in the Roman Empire who practiced polytheism or ethnic religion other than Judaism.

Panspiritual - Relating to, or encompassing all kinds of spirituality.

Penance – Any act of or set of actions done out of repentance for sins. Penance derives from French and Latin paemtentia, meaning the desire to be forgiven.

Pilgrim- a person who journeys to a sacred place for religious reasons.

Polytheism – Belief in multi deities, usually assembled in a pantheon of gods and goddesses, along with their own religious sects and rituals.

Prayer – a solemn request for help or expression of thanks to God. Also, an object of worship.

PreDestination – Divine fordaining of all that will happen. Religious doctrine associated with St. Augustine of Hippo (and of Calvin).

Protestatism - the faith, practice, and Church order of the Protestant Churches.

Quran – Muslim Islamic text.

Reconciliation- Catholic sacrament involving the confession of sin.

Ramadan- Holy month of fasting. Nineth month of the Muslim calendar. Muslims over 12 fast from Dusk to Dawn, and give charity.

Rastafarianism- religion venerating Haile Selassie as a god by Black Jamaicans, teaching the eventual redemption of Black people and their return to Africa.

Reformation – Movement to reform the catholic church that led to the creation of Protestantism.

Religion- from the Latin "religae" which means to bind.

Rite of Acceptance – When an Inquirer is formally accepted by the Community as a Catechumen / Candidate celebrated anytime of the year during Mass.

Rite of Election- When a Cathechumen is received, the local Bishop, renamed as Elect. Only happens on the first Sunday of Lent. Ritual when all Catechumens and Candidates from the diocese join together.

Rosicrucians- the fraternity of the Rosy Cross began to exhert influence to counteract religious intolerance, remaining underground until publication of The ordes Manifesto in 1614.

Sacrastan/Sacristan- person in charge of where a Priest prepares for service or Mass, (aka Vestry)-**Sacristy**- in a church.

Sadhana- Daily Spiritual practice (Indian)

Saint (Who?)- person acknowledged as holy or virtuous and typically regarded as being in heaven after death.

Sanctification- ongoing growth in holiness.

Secular-being unrelated or neutral to religion and irreligion or non religion.

Schism, Great- break of communion betweenWestern and Eastern churches, in 1054.

Scholasticism – Medieval way of thinking that changed the study of theology.

Scripture-sacred writings of Christianity in the Bible.

Sign of the Cross- Catholic crossing oneself (Joining the first three fingers, symbolizing the Holy Trinity, and putting the two other fingers in the palm, then touching forehead, below the chest, left side, then right side and finishing with open hand on the chest again with bowing head).

Seminary school- teaches biblical studies and theology.

Sermon on the Mount - The Sermon delivered by Jesus to His disciples.

Shalom- "Peace" (Jewish).

Sin/Sinner- an immoral act against God or divine law. Person who transgresses against divine law.

Sponsor- A Catholic who has celebrated all the Sacraments of Initiation and is living in faith, who journeys with the Cathechumen/Elect.

Stations of the Cross-14 Step Catholic devotion that commemorates Jesus Christ's last day on Earth as a man.

Sufi - a Muslim who seeks annihilation of the ego in God.

Syllabus- a summary of points decided by Papal decree regarding heretical doctrines or practices in Catholic church.

Synagogue - building where Jews meet for religious worship and instruction.

Synod- assembly (from the Greek) of the clergy or council of a Christian denomination convened to decide an issue, doctrine or application.

Temple- building devoted to worship of God or Gods.

Theist- Opposite of an atheist. Believes in the existence of God or Gods.

Theology- study of the nature of God and religious belief.

Thich Nhat Hanh- Famed Vietnamese monk and Buddhist teacher.

Tilaka- mark (Sanskrit) on forehead (Hindu). Red dot.

Unity Church- founded on spiritual principles of healing. (Co founder Myrtle Fillmore was told she had 6 months to live. Turning to meditation and prayer, she lived to 86!).

Vestments-liturgical garments and articles associated with Christian religion, Eastern, Catholic, Anglican and Lutheran churches.

Vestry-where Priest changes into vestments.

Vicar-Priest with a Mission as opposed to a Parish.

Yoga- Union.

A MASS FOR YOUR INTENTIONS

May the Peace and Blessing of God Be Upon You and Remain With You Always.

For Further Reading to learn more, explore and understand:

- "Angelus," Published by the Roman Catholic Archdiocese of Los Angeles by The Tidings (a corporation) est. 1895. Subscription available.
- "This Is How You Pray," by Karen Brailsford, Unity Magazine.org November/December 2021 page 18

Fascinating booklet "21 Dangerous Prayers," by Gary Rohrmayer…*well* worth reading. Especially read page 26, Day 9, "O LORD, save me from whining!" It's great.

"How to Sit," by Thich Nhat Hanh, © 2014 The United Buddhist Church, Parallax Press,

"Our Daily Bread," Grow in your relationship with Jesus not in a half baked way. Free devotional booklet. www.odb.org

Peer Magazine, Salvation Army hip magazine. Full of great content and design. www.peermag.org

"The Holy Land Review (The Pilgrims Companion to the Land Where Jesus Walked)." Subscription available.

Inner Traditions Bear & Company, Books for the Mind, Body and Spirit. www.innertraditions.org

"Serenity," A beautiful pocket-sized book of inspirational verses and poems by various writers, compiled and edited by Sarah Tarascio. Illustrations by Marion L. Quimby and Paul Scully. Salesian Missions, New Rochelle, New York.

- Serra Retreat (Malibu) photos with permission,

- "Guard Me Oh Lord As The Apple of Your Eye" Illustration by Corita Kent.
- "Popemobile" Cartoon, Joe Heller ©
- "My Religion...Dalai Lama bumpersticker, © Syracuse Cultural Workers
- "Instrument of Peace"; "Buddha Nature"; "Signpost" (pen and ink by the author).
- "Percy the Postie" Cartoon by Doug Durich.
- "Intertwined" By John Conley.
- "Surrender" book cover, Bono, ©Anton Corbijn, Alfred A. Knopf, Publisher, New York, 2022.
- Cartoon, by Brenton.daily©
- **Steve** Kaufmann illustration. "Pop Mother and Child" Original- with permission, © Steve Kaufman Art Licensing LLC.
- Old Testament/New Testament bookmark.

Juggling hats as artist and writer, Gordon David Durich was hatched in Europe, raised in Australia, lived in London on and off (mostly) and moved to the US in the mid 1990's. Meeting his wife-to--be writer and PR pro Kitty Dill at the Santa Barbara Writers Conference. Their marriage turned his family - and world upside down, but it also introduced him to new thought and positive vibes.

He resides mostly in the Los Angeles area with his writer wife - and ever-obliging "publicist".

"Peace is a necessary condition of spirituality, no less than an inevitable result of it."
Aldous Huxley

PRINT MEDIA CREDITS & INSPIRATIONS

Own Our History: Change the Story, Brene Brown, (article) 2015.
Guideposts magazine, October 2018; page 11, **In Touch magazine**: page 15, **AARP magazine**, (February/March, 2022); page 16, "The Last Days of John Lennon," James Patterson, Casey Sherman and Dave Wedge, Little Brown and Company, New York, 2020; page 20, **"Rejuvenate: Looking Younger and Feeling Vital,"** Devra Z. Hill, Avery Publishing Group, New York, 1991; page 44,; **"A Plea for Serenity,"** by Gorda Jeffcoat, Salesian Inspirational Books, New York, 1983; page 68, **Edmonton Journal**: page 70, November/December 2021 issue of Unity magazine; page 75, **Lion's Roar magazine**; page 84, **New York Times**; **Readers Digest, October 2022**; **Peer Magazine**; **The Atlantic**.

"This my God is my prayer. Draw me from Your Fire, form me on Your anvil, shape me with your hands and let me be your tool." *Max Lucado.*

ELECTRONIC MEDIA CREDITS

Unity Online Radio show "The Intentional Spirit… Seeing, Hearing and Being." (Fanny Flagg interview with Rev. Temple Hayes, Nov. 2020).

Coast to Coast, KFI AM radio, George Noori host.

"On The Road to Find Out," *Cat Stevens,*
©Universal Music Group, 1970
"Everyday I Write The Book," *Elvis Costello,*
©BMG Rights Management, Universal Music
Publishing Group, 1983.
"I'm Free," *(Peter Townshend - Who), ©Decca,*
"Another Brick in the Wall," *(George) Rogers*
Waters- Pink Floyd, Lyrics©Roger Waters, Harvest
(UK)/Columbia (US), 1979.
"White Wedding," *Billy Idol, ©BMG Rights*
Management, 1982.
"God Save The Queen," *Glen Matlock, John Lydon,*
Paul Thomas Cook, Stephen Phillip Jones-Sex Pistols,
©BMG Rights Management, Universal Publishing
Group, Warner Chappell Music, Inc., 1977.
"Wedding Song (There is Love)," *Noel Paul*
Stookey, ©Warner Bros-Neworld Media, 1971.
"Day By Day," *John Michael Tebelak, Stephen*
Schwartz – Godspell, 1973.Lyrics © DistroKid 1971.
"Hair," *Galt McDermot, James Rado- Hair, 1967.*
"Enter The Sandman," *Metallica, Kirk Hammett,*
James Hetfield,Lars Ulrich, ©Word Collections
Publishing, Vertigo.

"Lost In Love," Air Supply Graham Russell, ©BMG Rights Management Group, Universal Music Publishing Group, 1979.

"Crippled Inside," John Lennon. ©Lenono Music, 1971.

"California Dreamin'," John Edmund Andrew Phillips and Michelle Gillam Phillips, Lyrics, © Universal Publishing Group, 1965.

"Vincent," Don McLean, ©Lyrics Songs of Universal Inc. Benny Bird Co. Inc. 1971.

"I Still Haven't Found What I'm Looking For," Paul David Hewson (Bono), Adam Clayton, Larry Mullen, Dave Evans – U2, Lyrics©Polygram Int Music Publishing B.v. Island, 1987.

"Space Oddity," David Bowie. Onward Music, Tro-Essex Music, Westminster Music & Essex Music (Publishers).©

"Peace I leave with you;
My Peace I give to you.
Not as the World gives do I give to you.
Let not your hearts be troubled, neither let them be
afraid."
- Jesus   (John 14:27)

INCLUDING   BIOGRAPHIES,   MEMOIRS   AND
CONVERSATIONS . . .

"Knowledge from books; wisdom from Life."
Jewish proverb

"The Book of Genesis" A New Translation from the
Transparent English Bible and James D. Taybor Genesis
2000 Press. 2020, Las Vegas 2022.
"The Purpose-Driven Life:What on Earth Am I Here For?"
Rick Warren, Zondervan 2002.
"Pathways to Bliss," Joseph Campbell, New World Library,
2004.
"Jesus Under Seige," Dr. Gregory Boyd, Victor Books, 1995.
"The Case for Christ," Lee Strobel, Zondervan Publishing
House,Michigan 1998.
"Fire Starters. Daily Conversations with God," Ron Vietti,
2019.
"Eucharist," Bishop Robert Barron, Word on Fire Institute,
2021.
"The Cross and the Switchblade," Rev. David Wilkerson
(true tale about small town preacher who takes to ministry in
NYC), Berkley, 1986.
"Sacre Blues," Taras Grescoe, Macfarlane Walter & Ross,
Toronto, 2001.

"Autobiography of a Yogi," Paramhansa Yogananda, Self-Realization Fellowship 1998.

(Also, Audiobook on Audible.com the medium Mike Austin liked about Yogananda Paramhansa).

"Back to God, Away from Religion: The Joycentrix Way. A Joyful Alternative to Organized Religions," Gopi Menon, Amazon, 2021

"The Flame of Love," Clark H. Pinnock, InterVarsity Press, 1996

"Small Town Big Miracle," Bishop W.C. Martin, Focus on the Family/Amazon, 2022.

"How To Sit," Thich Nhat Hahn, The Unified Buddhist Church, Parallax Press, 2014

"The Biggest Lie in the History of Christianity," Matthew Kelly, Blue Sparrow Books, Florida 2018

"Inside Catholicism: Rituals and Symbols Revealed," Richard P. McBrien, (Signs of the Sacred) Collins Publishers, San Francisco, A Division of Harper Collins, 1995

"Quotes," Maharishi Mahash Yogi. Apple Books.

"A New Earth. Awakening to Your Life's Purpose," Eckhart Tolle, Spiritual Life. Plume Books/Penguin Books, London, 2005.

"Mere Christianity," C.S. Lewis, Harper Collins Publishers, 1980.

"No Compromise," Keith Green, Thomas Nelson, 2008.

"On the Outside Looking Up: Seeking and Following God…," Elizabeth Massie, Valley House Books, 2016.

"Only Nuns Change Habits Overnight," Karen Scalf Linamen, Waterbrook Press, Colorado 2008.

"The Four Signs of A Dynamic Catholic," Matthew Kelly, Beacon Publishing/The Dynamic Catholic Institute, KY. 2012.

"Chants of a Lifetime," Krisna Das, Audible Audiobook Hay House, 2021.

"Flame of Love," Clark H. Pinnock, IVP Academic, 2022.

"The Four Signs of a Dynamic Catholic," Matthew Kelly, Beacon Publishing, 2012.

"Jesus, Buddha, Krishna and Lao Tzu, " Richard Hooper, Sanctuary Publications, 2007.

"Jesus Calling… Enjoying Peace in His Presence," Sarah Young. Thomas Nelson, 2004. Devotions for *Every* Day of the Year.

"The Seven Storey Mountain," Thomas Merton, Houghton Mifflin, New York, 1998 (Harcourt, 1948)

"Stranger at the Gate: To Be Gay and Christian," Mel White, Plume, 1995.

"Life Without Limits,"Nick Vujicic, (also "Unstoppable: The Incredible Power of Faith in Action,") WaterBrook, 2012.

"More Together Than Alone," Discovering the Power and Spirit of Community in Our Lives and in the World," Mark Nepo, Atria Books, 2018.

"Surrender," Bono, Alfred A. Knopf, New York, 2022.

"There is A God: How The World's Most Notorious Atheist Changed His Mind," Antony Flew, Harper Collins, New York 2007

"Y'Shua- The Jewish Way to Say Jesus," Moishe Rosen, Moody Press, Chicago, 1982

"The Aquarian Conspiracy," Marilyn Ferguson, Tarcher Perigree, New York City, 2009.

"Only Nuns Can Change Their Habits Overnight…" Karen Scalf Linamen, WaterBrook, 2008.

"What's So Amazing About Grace?" Philip Yancey, Zondervan, New York, 2002.

"The Art of Happiness," His Holiness The Dalai Lama and Howard C. Cutler, Riverhead Books, a member of Penguin Putnam Inc. New York, 1998

"I Forgot to Die," and "Remembering to Live") Khalil Rafati, Lionscrest Publishing, 2015 (Paperback and E Book).

"Faith, Hope and Carnage," Nick Cave and Sean O'Hagan, Farrar, Strauss and Giroux, New York, 2022.

"A Bold Fresh Piece of Humanity," Bill O'Reilly, Broadway Books, New York, 2008.

"Strong Memory Sharp Mind," Frank Minirth, MD, Revell, a division of Baker Publishing Group, 2017

"Sting and Religion: The Catholic Shaped Imagination of a Rock Icon." Evytar Mariensberg, Cascade, 2021.

"Creating the Beloved Community: A Handbook for Spiritual Leadership (Book 1)," Being the Beloved Community: Spiritual Leadership to Master Change" (Book 2); Jim Lockard, Oneness Books/Amazon, 2017;2022.

"Common Phrases and Where They Came From," Myon Korach with John Mordock, Second Edition, The Lyons Press, Guilford, Connecticut, an imprint of the Globe Pequout Press, 2008

"Luck or Something Like It: A Memoir," Kenny Rogers (discusses his religious upbringing). Willm Morrow Paperbacks, 2013

"The Shamanic Powers of Rolling Thunder as Experienced by Alberto Villoldo et al," Edited by Sidian Morning Star Jones (Rolling Thunder's grandson) et al., Bear & Company, Rochester, Vermont, 2016. (Read "Sensing Rolling Thunder's Energy," by Michael D. Austin (my bro-in-law). His Dalai Lama meeting.

"Health from God's Garden," Marian Treben, Inner Traditions, 2022.

"Best Vacation Ever: The Ultimate Travel Guide…" Thor Challgren, Flying Lessons Press, 2022.

"STRONGER: Forty Days of Metal and Spirituality" Brian "Head" Welch, Harper One, an imprint of Harper Collins Publishers, New York 2010

"A Question of Yams," a missionary story based on true events, by Gloria Repp. Set in Papua New Guinea. How a young boy learned to trust the "one true God." For any age. Journey Forth /BJU Press, Greenville, South Carolina, 1992.

"Eat Pray Love," Elizabeth Gilbert, Riverhead Books, 2007. www.elizabethgilbert.com/eat-pray-love

"The Magic of Believing," Claude Bristol, Ixia Press, 2019 (reissue). Positive thoughts lead to miracles!

"You Are Enough: Always Have Been, Always Will Be," David Walker, DeVorss Publications, Camarillo, 2007.
"The Chiffon Trenches A Memoir," Andre Leon Talley, Ballantine Books, New York, 2021.
…And, last but not least, "The 5 Questions," Dr. James Mellon, MB Artists/Amazon, 2023. Profound new thought.

"SIT FINIS LIBRI, NON FINIS QUAERENDI"...
(This May Be The End of the Book, but the Beginning of the Search)

ΩΩ

EDITOR
Shari Hollander

LAYOUT AND DESIGN
John Conley

Front and Back Cover
John Conley

USA   2024

Made in the USA
Las Vegas, NV
23 March 2024

87669276R00079